Thomas Edgar Pemberton

Charles Dickens and the Stage

A Record of his Connection with the Drama as Playwright, Actor, and Critic

Thomas Edgar Pemberton

Charles Dickens and the Stage
A Record of his Connection with the Drama as Playwright, Actor, and Critic

ISBN/EAN: 9783744678070

Printed in Europe, USA, Canada, Australia, Japan

Cover: Foto ©ninafisch / pixelio.de

More available books at **www.hansebooks.com**

CHARLES DICKENS
AND
THE STAGE

A RECORD
OF HIS CONNECTION WITH THE DRAMA AS PLAYWRIGHT ACTOR
AND CRITIC.

BY

T EDGAR PEMBERTON,

Author of " Dickens's London.

WITH NEW PORTRAITS IN CHARACTER OF

MISS JENNIE LEE, MR. IRVING, AND MR. TOOLE.

LONDON:
GEORGE REDWAY, YORK ST., COVENT GARDEN
1888.

PRINTED BY
KELLY AND CO., GATE STREET, LINCOLN'S INN FIELDS,
AND KINGSTON-ON-THAMES.

CONTENTS.

CHAP.	PAGE
I.—Introductory	1
II.—The Stage in his Novels	5
III.—Dickens as a Dramatist	79
IV.—Dickens as an Actor	96
V.—Adaptations and Impersonations	136
VI.—The Stage in his Speeches	186
VII.—The Stage in his Letters	201
VIII.—Dickens as a Dramatic Critic	232
IX.—Conclusion	246

DICKENS AND THE STAGE.

DICKENS AND THE STAGE.

CHAPTER I.

INTRODUCTORY.

It has often been said that in gaining a great novelist the English-speaking world lost an almost unequalled actor, and a most powerful dramatist; in other words, that if, instead of devoting himself to the writing of fiction in volume form, Charles Dickens had identified himself with the stage, he would have made upon it, both as performer and as writer, a name second to none in theatrical history. The question is hardly to be argued. By the interpretation of parts undertaken in amateur performances, and still more notably by the extraordinary dramatic power which he evinced at the reading desk, and by means of which he was able, alone, and unaided by scenery or other stage surroundings, to hold, spellbound, critical audiences, and at his will to call forth tears or laughter, Dickens proved that as an actor he was the possessor of absolute genius. To judge of his powers as a dramatist by the little plays that are fathered with his name would be manifestly absurd. It cannot be said that any one of them possesses distinctive dramatic merit; but all were the work of his 'prentice hand, written, probably, at a time when he was anxious and willing to write anything that would be likely to bring him before the public and to set him going on a much coveted literary career; and it is quite certain that all would have been forgotten had they not been associated with the name of "Boz." It is quite likely, indeed, that it was the magic of that name, though then only in its infancy, that induced London managers to accept and produce such trivialities as "The Strange Gentleman," "The Village Coquettes" and "Is She His Wife; or, Something Singular." At about the time when this last-named "burletta" received bold advertisement as a "newly-discovered play by Charles Dickens," the compiler of these pages witnessed its representation on the stage. It was well performed, the part of Mr. Limbury being in especially competent hands, but notwithstanding its authorship, it entirely failed to excite either interest, laughter or applause, and it is exceedingly doubtful whether Dickens would have been grateful to those who, with the honest intention of doing honour to his name, had resuscitated the dramatic work of his inexperienced days. Why, it is often asked, did not our novelist in his best days contribute to the dramatic literature of his time? The answer, to those who have any experience in such matters, seems simple enough. Would anyone who had such absolute command of the reading world prefer to write for the stage, when, in edition rapidly succeeding edition, his work found eager demand in book form? Would Shakespeare have immortalised his great ideas in scenes and acts, to be interpreted (or misinterpreted) by the players of all time, if there had in his day existed a Messrs. Chapman & Hall, to produce them as Dickens's works were produced? Think for one moment of the saving in time, and in wear and tear of mind and body, that the novelist has over the dramatist, and then ask why Dickens elected to be the one rather than the other. Seated in the seclusion of his comfortable study, the skilled and popular novelist conjures up his characters, word-paints his scenes, sends his manuscript to the publisher, corrects his proofs, and knows, at least, that his creations will be read as they have by him been thought out. There are no delays in consulting this or that theatrical manager as to whether his work is suitable for the particular theatre which he governs; no doubts as to whether it is in touch with the prevailing fashion of the moment; no perplexities as to the suitable casting of the characters; no scene-painter or stage-carpenter to be consulted; no wearisome rehearsals to be attended; no first-night agonies to be undergone; no too hastily-written criticisims to be read. Happy enough must be the successful dramatist, but happier far the favourite novelist. It must be remembered, too, that even so short a time ago as the days of Dickens, the English stage was not the stage of to-day. Not only was the reward of the playwright a far smaller one, but (those who deplore the palmy days of the drama notwithstanding) the chances of getting his work brilliantly interpreted and artistically staged were infinitely less. Dickens, at the age of forty, devoting his genius to the London stage of 1887 is a thing for the theatre-lover to lie and dream about. But though his brilliant pen was not directed to the writing of sparkling comedy dialogue—to the imbroglio of rollicking farce,—or to the conjuring up of soul-stirring melodrama—his keen interest in the theatre and his vivid knowledge of it and its surroundings from every point of view, were features in his life, and bright and welcome streams running through his inimitable contributions to English literature. Such being the case, it seems worth while to the writer—and he hopes that his view will be shared by his readers—to linger for awhile within the pleasant precincts of Dickens's stageland.

CHAPTER II.

THE STAGE IN HIS NOVELS.

PROBABLY the first mention of "things theatrical" made in Dickens's published writings, is in that chapter in the delightful "Sketches by Boz," entitled "Private Theatres," and which commences as follows:—

"Richard the Third, Duke of Glo'ster, £2; Earl of Richmond, £1; Duke of Buckingham, 15s.; Catesby, 12s.; Tressell, 10s. 6d.; Lord Stanley, 5s.; Lord Mayor of London, 2s. 6d."

"Such are the written placards wafered up in the gentlemen's dressing-room, or the greenroom (where there is any), at a private theatre; and such are the sums extracted from the shop till, or over-charged in the office expenditure, by the donkeys who are prevailed upon to pay for permission to exhibit their lamentable ignorance and boobyism on the stage of a private theatre. This they do in proportion to the scope afforded by the character for the display of their imbecility. For instance, the Duke of Glo'ster is well worth two pounds, because he has it all to himself; he must wear a real sword, and, what is better still, he must draw it several times in the course of the piece. The soliloquies alone are well worth fifteen shillings; then there is the stabbing King Henry—decidedly cheap at three and six pence, that's eighteen and six pence; bullying the coffin bearers—say eighteen pence, though it's worth much more, that's a pound. Then the love scene with Lady Ann, and the bustle of the fourth act, can't be dear at ten shillings more—that's only one pound ten, including the 'off with his head!' which is sure to bring down the applause— and it is very easy to do—'Orf with his 'ed' (very quick and loud; then slow and sneeringly)—'So much for B-u-u-uckingham.' Lay the emphasis on the 'uck'; get yourself gradually into a corner, and work with your right hand, while you're saying it, as if you were feeling your way, and it's sure to do. The tent scene is confessedly worth half-a-sovereign, and so you have the fight in, gratis, and everybody knows what an effect may be produced by a good combat."

Luckily we do not, now-a-days, hear much of these private theatres, the principal patrons of which were, according to Dickens, " dirty boys, low copying clerks in attorney's offices, capacious headed youths from city counting-houses, Jews, whose business as lenders of fancy dresses is a sure passport to the amateur stage, shop-boys, who now and then mistake their master's money for their own; and a choice miscellany of idle vagabonds"; but the "donkeys—who pay for permission to exhibit their lamentable ignorance on the stage," find a ready outlet in the present *matinée* system. How many an immature Juliet (I beg her pardon, she generally, I think, prefers to pose as the heroine of " La Dame aux Camélias), how many a would-be emulator of Irving has paid dearly for the privilege of figuring at an afternoon performance at a London theatre, only to prove that the stage is the very last vocation that she, or he, should follow. But the would-be dramatist is in this respect an even greater sinner than the amateur actress or actor. How many hopeless failures have during the past few years been brought under the notice of a helpless public at *matinées?* How many hundreds, nay thousands, of pounds, must in this way have been squandered! It would have been well, indeed, for many an over-confident author if the theatre in which his utter incompetence has been made manifest had been a " private one."

To return to the private theatres of " Boz," however, we find that the " Jenkinses, Walkers, Thomsons, Barkers, Solomons, etc," who disport themselves on the boards thereof had a singular (?) habit of assuming for stage purposes such names as " Belville, Melville, Treville, Berkeley, Randolph, Byron, and St. Clair," and we are given a glimpse behind the scenes prior to a performance of "Macbeth." "The little narrow passages beneath the stage are neither especially clean nor too brilliantly lighted; and the absence of any flooring, together with the damp, mildewy smell which pervades the place, does not conduce in any great degree to their comfortable appearance. Don't fall over this plate-basket, it's one of the 'properties'—the caldron for the witches' cave; and the three uncouth-looking figures, with broken clothes-props in their hands, who are drinking gin-and-water out of a pint pot, are the weird sisters. . . . . . . That snuff-shop-looking figure in front of the glass is Banquo; and the young lady with the miserable display of legs, who is kindly painting his face with a hare's foot, is dressed for Fleance. The large woman, who is consulting the stage directions in Cumberland's edition of 'Macbeth,' is the Lady Macbeth of the night . . . . . That stupid milksop, with light hair and bow legs—a kind of man whom you can warrant town-made—is fresh caught; he plays Malcolm to-night, just to accustom himself to an audience. He will get on better by degrees; he will play Othello in a month, and in a month more will very probably be apprehended on a charge of embezzlement. The black-eyed female, with whom he is talking so earnestly, is dressed for the 'gentle-woman.' It is *her* first appearance, too—in that character. The boy of fourteen, who is having his eyebrows smeared with soap and whitening, is Duncan, King of Scotland; and the two dirty men with the corked countenances, in very old green tunics and dirty drab boots, are the ' army.' "

Humorous as is this grim description there is about it an unsavoury squalor, and a sense of degradation to Shakespeare and the drama, which, however true it may have been, makes one turn with a sigh of relief even to the expensive, the wearisome, and the much abused, semi-amateur *matinée* of to-day. With positive delight one turns from it to the delightful sketch on drawing-room theatricals which the same volume contains, and which is known to every one under its title of "Mrs. Joseph Porter." It is needless to say much here of that famous amateur representation of "Othello," which was given in the house of Mr. Gattleton, of Clapham Rise, in which a delay was occasioned by the detention of Iago at his duties in the Post Office; in which none of the performers could walk in their tights, or move their arms in their jackets; in which the pantaloons were too small, the boots too large, and the swords of all shapes and sizes; in which the Roderigo, naturally too tall for the scenery, wore a black velvet hat with immense.

white plumes, the glory of which was lost in "the flies"; and the only other inconvenience of which was, that when it was off his head he could not put it on, and when it was on he could not take it off; in which this same unlucky Roderigo fell with his head and shoulders as neatly through one of the side scenes, as a harlequin would jump through a panel in a Christmas pantomime; and of all of which, and much more, critical and ill-natured Mrs. Joseph Porter made abundant fun, and, alas! so much mischief with wealthy Uncle Tom. Many of us have witnessed the ludicrous and almost pitiable absurdities of these primitive amateur theatrical performances; some of us (let it with contrition be confessed!) have even gone so far as to take part in them, and it is very certain that on each and every occasion that such an entertainment (?) is given, there is, among the audience, a Mrs. Joseph Porter. Let one word be said in favour of the Gattleton family. They did not air their incompetence in public, they did not give their performance on behalf of "a charity." All honour to the Gattletons for confining their "acting" to the Theatre Royal, Back Drawing Room. Shame upon you, Mrs. Joseph Porter, for being under such circumstances so captious. A Mrs. Joseph Porter, who has been bullied into paying five shillings for a ticket, has earned a manifest right to say, and do, what she pleases.

Before taking leave of " The Sketches " mention must not be omitted of the delightful chapter entitled "Astley's" (Kit and Barbara with their mothers and Little Jacob had, later on, a right royal evening there you will remember), and in which " Boz " says:—" We should very much like to see some piece in which all the dramatis personæ were orphans. Fathers are invariably great nuisances on the stage, and always have to give the hero or heroine a long explanation of what was done before the curtain rose, usually commencing with, 'It is now nineteen years, my dear child, since your blessed mother (here the old villain's voice falters) confided you to my charge. You were then an infant, etc., etc.' Or else they have to discover, all of a sudden, that somebody whom they have been in constant communication with, during three long acts, without the slightest suspicion, is their own child; in which case they exclaim, ' Ah, what do I see ? This bracelet! That smile! These documents! Those eyes! Can I believe my senses? It must be! Yes—it is, it is my child!' 'My father,' exclaims the child; and they fall into each other's arms, and look over each other's shoulders, and the audience give three rounds of applause."

In "The Pickwick Papers" the drama is chiefly represented by that amusing vagabond, Mr. Alfred Jingle, who, albeit not an ornament to his profession, was, no doubt, in his own line of business, a very excellent actor. And here it seems worth while to note that, while Dickens saw all that was amusing, grotesque, tawdry, and even humiliating, in some phases of theatrical life, he touched the subject with so delicate and humorous a hand, that not even the most ardent stickler for the honour of the actor and the position of his art can take exception to it. Proof of this is amply found in the fact that out of the character of this graceless and impudent strolling player, whose life was certainly not one to add lustre to the theatrical profession, Mr. Henry Irving has found one of his most brilliantly successful comedy impersonations. Other writers who have from time to time, with heavier hand and less delicacy of perception, endeavoured in their books to make capital out of the "truth about the stage"—in other words, to speak of that seamy side which, in common with every other art, profession, or business by which men and women make a living, the theatre can present—have only given offence to its best advocates and annoyance to an outside public unanxious to be enlightened on such subjects. Dickens, on the other hand, whether he is speaking of the rascality of Jingle, the absurdities of the Crummles family, the pretensions of Mr. Wopsle, or the degradation of poor old Frederick Dorrit, only makes one smile and sigh and think in a kindly spirit of an institution to which the majority of us are inestimably indebted.

It was to Mr. Jingle, it will be remembered, that Mr. Pickwick and his friends were under obligations for the introduction to Mr. Jem Hutley, otherwise known as " dismal Jemmy "—" rum fellow—does the heavy business—no actor—strange man—all sorts of miseries "—and it was that same " Dismal Jemmy" who, having declared that "to be before the footlights is like sitting at a grand Court show, and admiring the silken dresses of the gaudy throng; to be behind them is to be the people who make that finery, uncared for and unknown, and left to sink or swim, to starve or live, as fortune wills it," related to the Pickwickians "The Stroller's Tale." The Consumptive Clown who is the unsavoury hero of this ghastly story, has become a somewhat hackneyed subject for ephemeral fiction (to the would-be writer of sensational romance, the combination of bismuth and hectic flush, gas glare and pneumonia, a laughing audience and a lungless comedian, are tantalizing materials), and except that some fine passages occur in his memoir, the history of the broken-down and drunken "John" might well be omitted from these pages. Here, however, are some theatrical lines that are too good to be passed over:—

"Everybody who is at all acquainted with theatrical matters knows what a host of shabby, poverty-stricken men hang about the stage of a large establishment — not regularly engaged actors, but ballet people, procession men, tumblers, and so forth, who are taken on during the run of a pantomime or an Easter piece, and are then discharged, until the production of some heavy spectacle occasions a new demand for their services." To this unfortunate class the hapless and dissolute "John" belonged, and the outcome of his wretched life was the horrible death, in which Dickens united his pen with the pencil of Seymour to make memory-haunting. It is no wonder that, having been associated with such scenes, the dismal Mr. Hutley should, as he leant with Mr. Pickwick over the balustrades of Rochester Bridge (on the destruction of the old bridge one of these balustrades became a garden fixture at Gad's Hill), opine that, "The calm, cool water seems to me to murmur an invitation to repose and rest. A bound, a splash, a brief struggle; there is an eddy for an instant, it gradually subsides into a gentle ripple; the waters have closed above your head, and the world has closed upon your miseries and misfortunes for ever!"

A far more wholesome and authentic picture of theatrical life, and of the clown's life in particular, is to be found in the delightful pages of the "Memoirs of Joseph Grimaldi," edited by "Boz," a work which might alone stand in evidence of Dickens's intense interest in the stage. To quote from "Grimaldi," would be an unnecessary and superfluous task. It is a theatrical classic that should be familiar to every stage-student.

Dickens is said to have held this work in very light estimation, and to have spoken of the material which in general composed it as "twaddle," but the warmth with which he resented an objection to his handling the subject on the ground that he could never have seen Grimaldi, shows that it must have had a place in his affections. "I understand," he wrote, "that a gentleman unknown is going about this town, privately informing all ladies and gentlemen of discontented natures, that, on a comparison of dates and putting together of many little circumstances which occur to his great sagacity, he has made the profound discovery that I can never have seen Grimaldi, whose life I have edited, and that the book must therefore of necessity be bad. Now, although I was brought up from remote country parts in the dark ages of 1819 and 1820 to behold the splendour of Christmas pantomimes and the humour of Joe, in whose honour, I am informed, I clapped my hands with great precocity, and although I even saw him act in the remote times of 1823; yet as I had not then aspired to the dignity of a tail coat, though forced by a relentless parent into my first pair of boots, I am willing, with the view of saving this honest gentleman further time and trouble, to concede that I had not arrived at man's estate when Grimaldi left the stage, and that my recollections of his acting are, to my loss, but shadowy and imperfect. Which confession I now make publicly, and without mental qualification or reserve, to all whom it may concern. But the deduction of this pleasant gentleman, that therefore the Grimaldi book must be bad, I must take leave to doubt. I don't think that to edit a man's biography from his own notes, it is essential you should have known him, and I don't believe that Lord Braybrooke had more than the very slightest acquaintance with Mr. Pepys, whose memoirs he edited two centuries after he died."

At this period Dickens's mind must have been much turned towards the stage, for in writing to his friend, Mr. John Forster, he says:—
"Talking of comedies, I still see No THOROUGH-

fare staring me in the face, every time I look down that road,"—and "the allusion to the comedy," remarks Mr. Forster, " expresses a fancy he, at this time, had of being able to contribute some such achievement in aid of Macready's gallant efforts at Covent Garden to bring back to the stage its higher asssociations of literature and intellectual enjoyment. It connects curiously now, that unrealised hope with the exact title of the only story he ever helped himself to dramatise, and which Mr. Fechter played at the Adelphi, three years before his death."

It was to Macready, too, "as a slight token of admiration and regard," that Dickens inscribed the pages of his next novel, the delightful "Nicholas Nickleby," wherein that famous group of theatrical characters who gathered around the standard of Mr. Vincent Crummles, were introduced to the world. Every line that is written about Mr. Crummles and his followers is instinct with good-natured humour, and from the moment when, in the road-side inn, "yet twelve miles short of Portsmouth," the reader comes into contact with the kindly old "circuit" manager, he finds himself in the best of good company. The key-note to the character of Mr. Crummles is sounded in the very first words that are written concerning him. "Mr. Vincent Crummles received Nicholas with an inclination of the head, something between the courtesy of a Roman Emperor and the nod of a pot companion," and then proceeded with the rehearsal of that terrific stage combat, in which "the short sailor made a vigorous cut at the tall sailor's legs, which would have shaved them clean off had it taken effect," whereupon "the tall sailor jumped over the short sailor's sword, wherefore to balance the matter, and make it all fair, the tall sailor administered the same cut, and the short sailor jumped over *his* sword. After this, there was a good deal of dodging about, and hitching up of the inexpressibles in the absence of braces, and then the short sailor (who was the moral character evidently, for he always had the best of it), made a violent demonstration, and closed with the tall sailor, who, after a few unavailing struggles, went down, and expired in great torture as the short sailor put his foot upon his breast, and bored a hole in him through and through."

What a delightful summing-up of the old-fashioned broadside fight of the stage is this, and what, in its way, could be more perfect than the indignant reply of Mr. Crummles to Nicholas's unsophisticated remark that he thought the effect would have been better if the combatants had been a " little more of a size."

" Size ! " repeated Mr. Crummles ; " why, it is the

essence of the combat that there should be a foot or two between them. How are you to get up the sympathies of an audience in a legitimate manner if there isn't a little man contending against a big one—unless there's at least five to one—and we haven't hands enough for that business in our company."

Theatrical economy such as this, and necessarily enforced stage expedients resulting thereupon, should surely be borne in mind by the too exacting critic.

It is soon after this that the managerial eye of Mr. Crummles becomes fascinated with the terribly worn and emaciated appearance of the unhappy Smike, who would, he declared, "without a pad upon his body, and hardly a touch of paint upon his face, make such an actor for the starved business as was never seen in this country. Only let him be tolerably well up in the Apothecary in 'Romeo and Juliet,' with the slightest possible dab of red on the tip of his nose, and he'd be certain of three rounds the moment he put his head out of the practicable door in the front grooves O.P."

A professional engagement with this extraordinary attraction, and with Nicholas, having been made, Mr. Crummles dilates to the latter upon his duties as dramatic author to the company.

"We'll have a new show-piece out directly," said the manager. "Let me see—peculiar resources of this establishment—new and splendid scenery—you must manage to introduce a real pump and two washing tubs."

"Into the piece?" said Nicholas.

"Yes," replied the manager. "I bought 'em cheap, at a sale the other day, and they'll come in admirably. That's the London plan. They look up some dresses, and properties, and have a piece written to fit 'em. Most of the theatres keep an author on purpose."

Nobody can for one moment imagine or suggest that that is nowadays the "London plan," but budding dramatists, who are anxious to obtain a hearing at any cost, and under any management, may still find themselves occasionally brought into contact with the managerial pump and tubs. He may think himself lucky, too, if these articles are always of an inanimate nature. The request to write another "speaking part" into a play upon which he has already expended his best efforts, is among the most trying ordeals that the experienced and uninfluential stage author has to undergo.

"And what should I get for all this?" inquired Nicholas, after he had received his instructions about writing the play, the important part that he would be expected to play in it, and an expression of regret that he was unable to undertake the designing of wood-cuts and posters. "Could I live by it?"

"Live by it?" said the manager. "Like a prince! With your own salary, and your friend's, and your writings, you'd make—Ah! you'd make a pound a week!"

Certainly in the days when Charles Dickens wrote "Nicholas Nickleby" there was little inducement for the young author to dabble in stage work. Dramatists of our time, or, at all events, the well known and successful ones, have another and a pleasanter tale to tell.

Determined to try his luck, however, Nicholas cast in his lot with Mr. Crummles, and accompanying him to Portsmouth, "turned into an entry, in which there was a strong smell of orange peel and lamp oil, with an under-current of sawdust, groped through a dark passage, and, descending a step or two, threaded a little maze of canvas screens and paint pots, and emerged upon the stage of the Portsmouth Theatre."

"Here we are," said Mr. Crummles.

"It was not very light, but Nicholas found himself close to the first entrance on the prompt side, among bare walls, dusty scenes, mildewed clouds, heavily daubed draperies, and dirty floors. He looked about him; ceiling, pit, boxes, gallery, orchestra, fittings, and decorations of every kind, all looked coarse, cold, gloomy, and wretched."

"Is this a theatre?" whispered Smike, in amazement. "I thought it was a blaze of light and finery!"

"Why, so it is," replied Nicholas, "but not by day, Smike—not by day."

In his "About England with Dickens," Mr. Alfred Rimmer gives a very interesting illustration of the exterior of the Portsmouth Theatre as it appeared in the days of Mr. Vincent Crummles.

Here, on the stage, and during the rehearsal of the little ballet interlude entitled "The Indian Savage and the Maiden," Nicholas made the acquaintance of Mrs. Crummles, of Miss Ninetta Crummles (otherwise known as the Infant Phenomenon), and of the other members of the Crummles company which, it will be remembered, included Mr. Folair, the pantomimist; Mr. Lenville, who "did first tragedy"; "a slim young gentleman with weak eyes, who played the low-spirited lovers, and sang tenor songs, and who had come arm-in-arm with the comic countryman"; "an inebriated elderly gentleman in the last depths of shabbiness, who played the calm and virtuous old men"; "another elderly gentleman, a shade more respectable, who played the irascible old men—those funny fellows who have nephews in the army, and perpetually run about with thick sticks to compel them to marry heiresses"; a roving-looking person in a rough greatcoat, who was the hero of swaggering comedy; Miss Snevellicci, "who could do anything, from a medley dance to Lady Macbeth, and also always played some part in blue silk knee smalls at her benefit"; Miss Belvawney, "who seldom aspired to speaking parts, and usually went on as a page in white silk hose, to stand with one leg bent, and contemplate the audience, or go in and out after Mr. Crummles in stately tragedy"; Miss Ledbrook; Miss Bravassa — the beautiful Miss Bravassa — "who had once had her likeness taken 'in character' by an engraver's apprentice, whereof impressions were hung up for sale in the pastrycook's window, and the greengrocer's, and at the circulating library, and the box-office, whenever the announce-bills came out for her annual night"; Mrs. Lenville, "decidedly in that way in which she would wish to be if she truly loved Mr. Lenville"; Miss Gazingi, and Mrs. Grudden, "who assisted Mrs. Crummles in her domestic affairs, and took money at the doors, and dressed the ladies, and swept the house, and held the prompt-book when everybody else was on for the last scene, and acted any kind of part in any emergency without ever learning it, and was put down in the bills under any name or names whatever that occurred to Mr. Crummles as looking well in print."

With a company so constituted it will be readily understood that Nicholas's position as playwright was fraught with perplexities. They were soon to commence.

"Is there anything good for me?" enquired Mr. Folair anxiously.

"Let me see," said Nicholas, "you play the faithful and attached servant; you are turned out of doors with the wife and child."

"Always coupled with that infernal Phenomenon," sighed Mr. Folair. "And we go into poor lodgings, where I won't take any wages, and talk sentiment, I suppose?"

"Why, yes," replied Nicholas, "that is in the course of the piece."

"I must have a dance of some kind, you know," said Mr. Folair. "You'll have to introduce one for the Phenomenon, so you'd better make it a *pas de deux*, and save time."

"There's nothing easier than that," said Mr. Lenville. . . . "You get the distressed lady, and the little child, and the attached servant, into the poor lodgings, don't you? Well, look here. The distressed lady sinks into a chair, and buries her face in her pocket-handkerchief. 'What makes you weep, Mamma?' says the child. 'Don't weep, Mamma, or you'll make me weep too!' 'And me,' says the faithful servant rubbing his eyes with his arm. 'What can we do to raise your spirits, dear Mamma?' says the little child. 'Aye, what *can* we do?' says the faithful servant. 'Oh, Pierre,' says the distressed lady, 'would that I could shake off these painful thoughts!' 'Try, Ma'am, try,' says the faithful servant; 'rouse yourself, Ma'am; be amused.' 'I will,' says the lady, 'I will learn to suffer with fortitude. Do you remember that dance, my honest friend, which, in happier days, you practised with this sweet angel? It never failed to calm my spirits then. Oh! let me see it once again before I die!' There it is, cue for the band, *before I die*—and off they go. That's the regular thing, isn't it, Tommy?"

"That's it," replied Mr. Folair. "The distressed lady, overpowered by old recollections, faints at the end of the dance, and you close in with a picture."

With his own part Mr. Lenville was better satisfied, and indeed, where is the "first tragedy" gentleman who could deny that to turn your wife and child out of doors; in a fit of rage and jealousy to stab your eldest son in the library; to be about to destroy yourself when the clock strikes ten; and then, remembering to have heard a clock strike ten in your infancy, to become remorseful and repentant; who can deny that all this is "very good business"?

But before the performance of his own adapted play, Nicholas was destined to witness one of the stock productions of Mr. Vincent Crummles, which is thus described:—

"The plot was most interesting. It belonged to no particular age, people, or country, and was perhaps the more delightful on that account, as nobody's previous information could afford the remotest glimmering of what would ever come of it. An outlaw had been very successful in doing something somewhere, and came home in triumph to the sound of shouts and fiddles, to greet his wife—a lady of masculine mind, who talked a good deal about her father's bones, which, it seemed, were unburied, though whether from a peculiar taste on the part of the old gentleman himself, or the reprehensible neglect of his relations, did not appear. This outlaw's wife was, somehow or other, mixed up with a patriarch living in a castle a long way off, and this patriarch was the father of several of the characters, but he didn't exactly know which, and was uncertain whether he had brought up the right ones in his castle or the wrong ones, but rather inclined to the latter opinion, and, being uneasy, relieved his mind with a banquet, during which solemnity somebody in a cloak said 'Beware!'

which somebody was known by nobody (except the audience) to be the outlaw himself, who had come there for reasons unexplained, but possibly with an eye to the spoons. There was an agreeable little surprise, in the way of certain love passages between the desponding captive and Miss Snevellicci, and the comic fighting-man and Miss Bravassa; besides which Mr. Lenville had several very tragic scenes in the dark, while on throat-cutting expeditions, which were all baffled by the skill and bravery of the comic fighting-man (who overheard whatever was said all through the piece) and the intrepidity of Miss Snevellicci, who adopted tights, and therein repaired to the prison of her captive lover, with a small basket of refreshments and a dark lantern. At last it came out that the patriarch was the man who had treated the bones of the outlaw's father-in-law with so much disrespect, for which cause and reason the outlaw's wife repaired to his castle to kill him, and so got into a dark room, where, after a good deal of groping in the dark, everybody got hold of everybody else, and took them for somebody besides, which occasioned a vast quantity of confusion, with some pistolling, loss of life, and torchlight; after which the patriarch came forward, and observing, with a knowing look, that he knew all about his children now, and would tell them when they got inside, said that there could not be a more appropriate occasion for marrying the young people than that; and therefore he joined their hands, with the full consent of the indefatigable page, who (being the only other person surviving) pointed with his cap into the clouds and his right hand to the ground; thereby invoking a blessing, and giving the cue for the curtain to come down, which it did, amidst general applause."

The production of Nicholas's initial dramatic effort was fixed for Miss Snevellicci's "bespeak night," and in accordance with a provincial custom then in vogue among minor theatrical companies, author and actress sallied forth to solicit the patronage of histrionically disposed Portsmouth. If only for the interview which the not too well-assorted pair had with Mr. and Mrs. Curdle of happy memory, the pilgrimage was well worth making.

"Now, Mrs. Curdle was supposed, by those who were best informed on such points, to possess quite the London taste in matters relating to literature and the drama; and as to Mr. Curdle, he had written a pamphlet of sixty-four pages, post octavo, on the character of the Nurse's deceased husband in 'Romeo and Juliet,' with an inquiry whether he really had been a 'merry man' in his lifetime, or whether it was merely his widow's affectionate partiality that induced her so to report him. He had likewise proved, that by altering the received mode of punctuation, any one of Shakespeare's plays could be made quite different, and the sense completely changed; it is needless to say, therefore, that he was a great critic, and a very profound and most original thinker."

Like most such self-appointed critics, Mr. Curdle was a great stickler for what are called the " unities " of the drama, and in response to an inquiry from Nicholas as to what he considered these same " unities " to be, he gave the following instructive, and hardly to be contradicted, definition.

" The unities, sir," he said, " are a completeness—a kind of universal dovetailedness with regard to place and time—a sort of general oneness, if I may be allowed to use so strong an expression. I take those to be the dramatic unities, so far as I have been able to bestow attention upon them, and I have read much upon the subject, and thought much. I find, running through the performances of this child," said Mr. Curdle, turning to the Phenomenon (it is needless to remind the reader that the young lady was present on the occasion), " a unity of feeling, a breadth, a light and shade, a warmth of colouring, a tone, a harmony, a glow, an artistical development of original conceptions, which I look for in vain, among older performers. I don't know whether I make myself understood."

"Perfectly," replied Nicholas.

It must be owned that Mr. Curdle's remarks contain some excellent stock phrases of which would-be critics of the present day are not slow to make use.

Very soon after this Miss Snevellicci took her benefit, Nicholas's pump-and-tub adaptation was produced with splendid success, and the happy dramatist was rewarded with " a presentation copy of Mr. Curdle's pamphlet, with that gentleman's own autograph (in itself an inestimable treasure) on the fly-leaf, accompanied with a note, containing many expressions of approval, and an unsolicited assurance that Mr. Curdle would be very happy to read Shakespeare to him for three hours every morning before breakfast during his stay in town."

And now it was that Miss Petowker, of the Theatre Royal, Drury Lane, joined the company; that same Miss Petowker who, notwithstanding her dislike to "doing anything professional at private parties," was good enough, within the sanctity of the Kenwigs' family circle, to recite " The Blood Drinker's Burial,"—to which end she " let down her back hair, and taking up her position at the other end of the room, with the bachelor friend posted in a corner, to rush out at the cue, ' in death expire,' and catch her in his arms when she died raving mad, went through the performance with extraordinary spirit."

"'The Blood Drinker' will die with that girl," said Mr. Crummles to Nicholas while they were discussing this important engagement, "and she's the only sylph *I* ever saw, who could stand upon one leg, and play the tambourine on her other knee, *like* a sylph."

But the estimation in which the worthy manager held the histrionic accomplishments of Miss Petowker was not to be outdone by the veneration with which he regarded the absolute genius of Mrs. Crummles. "I pledge you my professional word," said he, speaking of his wife, "I didn't even know she could dance till her last benefit, and then she played Juliet and Helen Macgregor, and did the skipping-rope hornpipe between the pieces. The very first time I saw that woman, she stood upon her head on the butt-end of a spear, surrounded with blazing fireworks."

Who that is familiar with them will ever forget, or fail to be grateful for, the humours of Mr. and Mrs. Crummles on the occasion of Miss Petowker's marriage to Mr. Lillyvick? for had not the manager, who personated the bride's father, " in pursuance of a happy and original conception 'made up' for the part by arraying himself in a theatrical wig, of a style and pattern commonly known as a brown George," and by " assuming a snuff-coloured suit of the previous century, with grey silk stockings, and buckles to his shoes?" "The better to support his assumed character," too, " he had determined to be greatly overcome, and, consequently, when they entered the church, the sobs of the affectionate parent were so heart-rending that the pew-opener suggested the propriety of his retiring to the vestry, and comforting himself with a glass of water before the ceremony began."

On her part Mrs. Crummles conducted herself with a stern and gloomy majesty, and advanced up the aisle "with that stage walk, which consists of a stride and a stop alternately," and it must not be forgotten that when it came to the signing of the registers Mr. Crummles "carefully wiped and put on an immense pair of spectacles."

That jealousy was not an unknown factor in the dramatic company of Mr. Crummles is shown by the challenge from Mr. Lenville which, "per favour of Mr. Folair," was conveyed to Nicholas, and by him received with contempt. "He cast about for some other way of annoying you," explained the abashed "Second," "and making himself popular at the same time—for that's the point. Notoriety, notoriety, is the thing. Bless you, if he had pinked you, it would have been worth—ah, it would have been worth eight or ten shillings a week to him. All the town would have come to see the actor who nearly killed a man by mistake," (this alluded to Mr. Lenville's intention to play "Tybalt" with a real sword). "I shouldn't wonder if it had got him an engagement in London. However, he was obliged to try some other mode of getting popular, and this one occurred to him. It's a clever idea, really. If you had shown the white feather, and let him pull your nose, he'd have got it into the paper; if you had sworn the peace against him, it would have been in the paper too, and he'd have been just as much talked about as you—don't you see?"

On Nicholas's declaring that he might have to leave the company, Mr. Crummles evinced many tokens of grief and consternation, but seeing there was no help for it he proceeded to look at the matter from a business point of view. "Let me see," he said, "This is Wednesday night. We'll have posters out the first thing in the morning, announcing positively your last appearance for to-morrow."

"But, perhaps it may not be my last appearance, you know," said Nicholas. "Unless I am summoned away, I should be sorry to inconvenience you by leaving before the end of the week."

"So much the better," returned Mr. Crummles. "We can have positively your last appearance on Thursday—re-engagement for one night more on Friday—and, yielding to the wishes of numerous influential patrons, who were disappointed in obtaining seats, on Saturday. That ought to bring three very decent houses."

"Then I am to make three last appearances, am I?" inquired Nicholas, smiling.

"Yes," rejoined the manager, scratching his head with an air of some vexation; "three is not enough, and it's very bungling and irregular not to have more, but if we can't help it we can't, so there's no use in talking. A novelty would be very desirable. You couldn't sing a comic song on the pony's back, could you?"

"No," replied Nicholas. "I couldn't indeed."

"It has drawn money before now," said Mr. Crummles, with a look of disappointment. "What do you think of a brilliant display of fireworks?"

"That would be rather expensive," replied Nicholas, drily.

"Eighteenpence would do it," said Mr. Crummles. "You on the top of a pair of steps with the phenomenon in an attitude; 'Farewell' on a transparency behind; and nine people at the wings with a squib in each hand—all the dozen and a half going off at once—it would be very grand—awful from the front, quite awful."

But before saying good-bye to Mr. Crummles and the Portsmouth Theatre, Nicholas had the honour of an introduction to Miss Snevellicci's papa, " who had been in the profession ever since he had first played the ten-year-old imps in the Christmas pantomimes; who could sing a little, dance a little, fence a little, act a little, and do everything a little but not much; who had been sometimes in the ballet, and sometimes in the chorus, at every theatre in London; who was always selected in virtue of his figure to play the military visitors and the speechless noblemen; who always wore a smart dress, and came in arm-in-arm with a smart lady in short petticoats, and always did it with such an air that people in the pit had been several times known to cry out 'Bravo!' under the impression that he was somebody. Such was Miss Snevillicci's papa, upon whom some envious persons cast the imputation that he occasionally beat Miss Snevellicci's mama, who was still a dancer, with a neat little figure, and some remains of good looks; and who now sat, as she danced—being rather too old for the glare of the footlights—in the back ground."

Miss Snevellicci's papa was gracious enough to compliment Nicholas upon his acting, saying that there hadn't been such a hit made—"no, not since the first appearance of his friend Mr. Glavormelly, at the Coburg."

"You have seen him, sir?" said Miss Snevellicci's papa.

"No, really, I never did," replied Nicholas.

"You never saw my friend Glavormelly, sir?" said Miss Snevellicci's papa, "then you have never seen acting yet. If he had lived——"

"Oh, he is dead, is he?" interrupted Nicholas.

"He is," said Mr. Snevellicci; "but he isn't in Westminster Abbey, more's the shame. He was a—well, no matter. He has gone to that bourne from whence no traveller returns. I hope he is appreciated *there*."

It was on the next day that the public were informed, "in all the colours of the rainbow, and in letters afflicted with every possible variation of spinal deformity, that Mr. Johnson" (otherwise Nicholas Nickleby) "would have the honour of making his last appearance that evening, and how that an early application for places was requested, in consequence of the extraordinary overflow attendant on his performances, it being a remarkable fact in theatrical history, but one long since established beyond dispute, that it is a hopeless endeavour to attract people to a theatre unless they can be first brought to believe that they can never get into it."

he entertainment was not only a great success in itself, but an unexpected lustre was added to it from the fact that a London manager was in the boxes.

"When everybody was dressed and the curtain went up, the excitement occasioned by the presence of the London manager increased a thousandfold. Everybody happened to know that the London manager had come down specially to witness his or her own performance, and all were in a flutter of anxiety and expectation. . . . Once the London manager was seen to smile—he smiled at the comic countryman's pretending to catch a blue-bottle, while Mrs. Crummles was making her greatest effect. 'Very good, my fine fellow,' said Mr. Crummles, shaking his fist at the comic countryman when he came off, 'you leave this company next Saturday night.'"

"In the same way, everybody who was on the stage beheld no audience but one individual; everybody played to the London manager. When Mr. Lenville, in a sudden burst of passion, called the emperor a miscreant, and then, biting his glove, said: 'But I must dissemble,' instead of looking gloomily at the boards and so waiting for his cue, as is proper in such cases, he kept his eyes fixed upon the London manager. When Miss Bravassa sang her song at her lover, who according to custom stood ready to shake hands with her between the verses, they looked, not at each other, but at the London manager. Mr. Crummles died point-blank at him; and when the two guards came in to take the body off after a very hard death, it was seen to open its eyes and glance at the London manager. At length the London manager was discovered to be asleep, and shortly after that he woke up and went away, whereupon all the company fell foul of the comic countryman, declaring that his buffoonery was the sole cause; and Mr. Crummles said that he had put up with it a long time, but that he really couldn't stand it any longer, and therefore would feel obliged by his looking out for another engagement."

After this, it will be remembered, Nicholas bade a final farewell to the stage, and it is not until we are nearly at the end of his history, and his lines have permanently fallen into other, if not more pleasant places, that Mr. Crummles again appears, "for positively the last time" upon the scene.

"Positively the last appearance of Mr. Vincent Crummles of Provincial Celebrity!!!" was, indeed, the announcement that met the eye of Nicholas as, in absent mood, he glanced at a play-bill hanging outside a minor London theatre.

"In one line by itself was an announcement

of the first night of a new melo-drama; in another line by itself was an announcement of the last six nights of an old one; a third line was devoted to the re-engagement of the unrivalled African knife-swallower, who had kindly suffered himself to be prevailed upon to forego his country engagements for one week longer; a fourth line announced that Mr. Snittle Timberry, having recovered from his late severe indisposition, would have the honour of appearing that evening; a fifth line said that there were 'Cheers, Tears, and Laughter!' every night; a sixth, that that was positively the last appearance of Mr. Vincent Crummles of Provincial Celebrity."

"Surely it must be the same man," thought Nicholas. "There can't be two Vincent Crummles"; and in a few moments he found himself in the managerial presence.

"Mr. Crummles was unfeignedly glad to see him, and starting up from before a small dressing-glass, with one very bushy eyebrow stuck on crooked over his left eye, and the fellow eyebrow and the calf of one of his legs in his hand, embraced him cordially, at the same time observing, 'that it would do Mrs. Crummles's heart good to bid him good-bye before they went.'"

"'But where are you going to that you talk about bidding good-bye?' asked Nicholas.

"'Haven't you seen it in the papers?' said Mr. Crummles, with some dignity.

"'No,' replied Nicholas.

"'I wonder at that,' said the manager; 'it was among the varieties. I had the paragraph here somewhere—but I don't know—oh, yes, here it is!'

"So saying Mr. Crummles, after pretending that he thought he must have lost it, produced a square inch of newspaper from the pantaloons he wore in private life, and gave it to Nicholas to read.

"'The talented Vincent Crummles, long favourably known to fame as a country manager and actor of no ordinary pretensions, is about to cross the Atlantic on a histrionic expedition. Crummles is to be accompanied, we hear, by his lady and gifted family. We know no man superior to Crummles in his particular line of character, or one who, whether as a public or private individual, could carry with him the best wishes of a larger circle of friends. Crummles is certain to succeed.'

"'Here's another bit,' said Mr. Crummles, handing over a still smaller scrap. 'This is from the notices to correspondents, this one.'

"Nicholas read it aloud:—

"'Philo Dramaticus.—Crummles, the country

manager and actor, cannot be more than forty-three or forty-four years of age. Crummles is NOT a Prussian, having been born in Chelsea.'

"'Humph!' said Nicholas, 'that's an odd paragraph.'

"'Very,' said Crummles, scratching the side of his nose, and looking at Nicholas with an assumption of great concern. 'I can't think who puts these things in. *I* didn't.'"

"Still keeping his eye on Nicholas, Mr. Crummles shook his head twice or thrice with profound gravity, and remarking that he could not for the life of him imagine how the newspapers found out the things they did, folded up the extracts and put them in his pocket again."

Nicholas was now informed that if he wished to take a last adieu of Mrs. Crummles, he must repair that night to a farewell supper, given in honour of the family at a neighbouring tavern, "at which Mr. Snittle Timberry would preside, while the honours of the vice-chair would be sustained by the African Swallower."

" It was upon the whole a very distinguished party, for independently of the lesser theatrical lights who clustered on this occasion round Mr. Snittle Timberry, there was a literary gentleman present, who had dramatised in his time two hundred and forty-seven novels, as fast as they came out—some of them faster than they had come out—and *was* a literary gentleman in consequence."

Nicholas expressed his gratification at meeting a person of such great distinction.

"'Sir,' replied the wit, 'you're very welcome, I'm sure. The honour is reciprocal, sir, as I usually say when I dramatise a book. Did you ever hear a definition of fame, sir?'"

"'I have heard several,' replied Nicholas with a smile. 'What is yours?'"

"'When I dramatise a book, sir,' said the literary gentleman, '*that's* fame — for its author.'"

"'Oh, inded!' rejoined Nicholas.

"'That's fame, sir,' said the literary gentleman.

"'So Richard Turpin, Tom King, and Jerry Abershaw, have handed down to fame the names of those on whom they committed their most impudent robberies,' said Nicholas.

"'I do not know anything about that, sir,' answered the literary gentleman.

"'Shakespeare dramatised stories which had previously appeared in print, it is true,' observed Nicholas.

"'Meaning Bill, sir?' said the literary gentleman. 'So he did. Bill was an adaptor, certainly, so he was—and very well he adapted, too, considering.'

"I was about to say,' rejoined Nicholas, 'that Shakespeare derived some of his plots from old tales and legends in general circulation; but it seems to me that some of the gentlemen of your craft of the present day have shot very far beyond him.'

"'You're quite right, sir,' interrupted the literary gentleman, leaning back in his chair and exercising his tooth-pick. 'Human intellect, sir, has progressed since his time—is progressing—will progress.'

"'Shot beyond him, I mean,' resumed Nicholas, 'in quite another respect, for whereas he brought within the magic circle of his genius traditions peculiarly adapted for his purpose, and turned familiar things into constellations which should enlighten the world for ages, you drag within the magic circle of your dulness, subjects not at all adapted to the purposes of the stage, and debase as he exalted. For instance, you take the uncompleted books of living authors, fresh from their hands, wet from the press, cut, hack and carve them to the powers and capacities of your actors, and the capability of your theatres, finish unfinished works, hastily and crudely vamp up ideas not yet worked out by their original projector, but which have doubtless cost him many thoughtful days and sleepless nights; by a comparison of incidents and dialogue, down to the very last word he may have written a fortnight before, do your utmost to anticipate his plot —all this without his permission and against his will; and then, to crown the whole proceeding, publish in some mean pamphlet an unmeaning farrago of garbled extracts from his work, to which you put your name as author, with the honourable distinction annexed of having perpetrated a hundred other outrages of the same description. Now, show me the distinction between such pilfering as this and picking a man's pocket in the street; unless, indeed, it be that the legislature has a regard for pocket handkerchiefs, and leaves men's brains, except when they are knocked out by violence, to take care of themselves.'

" ' Men must live, sir,' said the literary gentleman, shrugging his shoulders.

"' That would be an equally fair plea in both cases,' replied Nicholas, ' but if you put it upon that ground, I have nothing more to say than, if I were a writer of books, and you a thirsty dramatist, I would rather pay your tavern score for six months—large as it might be—than have a niche in the Temple of Fame with you for the humblest corner of my pedestal, through six hundred generations.'"

After this outburst one is scarcely surprised to read that " the conversation threatened to take a somewhat angry tone" (the subject of it was one on which Dickens had good cause to feel strongly, and, like many more injured men, he perhaps, as will be seen later on in these pages, hardly weighed the force of his remarks), but the "literary gentleman" was presumably a lover of peace, and not only did the banquet go off magnificently, but the subsequent and inevitable speech-making was a gratifiying success until the health of the literary gentleman himself had to be drunk, when "it being discovered that he had been drunk for some time in another acceptation of the term, and was then asleep on the stairs, the intention was abandoned, and the honour transferred to the ladies."

When the time came for Nicholas to bid farewell to the warm-hearted Vincent Crummles, "not a jot of the theatrical manner remained; he put out his hand with an air which, if he could have summoned it at will, would have made him the best actor of his day in homely parts, and when Nicholas shook it with the warmth he honestly felt, appeared thoroughly melted."

"'We were a very happy little company, Johnson,' said poor Crummles. 'You and I never had a word. I shall be very glad to-morrow morning to think that I saw you again, but now I almost wish you hadn't come.'"

Very briefly has the compiler of these pages

passed over the inimitable chapters in "Nicholas Nickleby," in which the Crummles family, and the Crummles company, do immortal service. Of course, since those days great advances in dramatic art have been made, and especially are provincial play-houses better provided with entertainment, but what was true of the minor theatre then, is more or less true of the minor theatre of to-day, and if in Dickens's descriptions exaggerations creep in, they may be forgiven a hundred times over for their humour. Certainly, at the present time we are not free from pretentious, self-constituted critics of the Curdle type; London managers are still in a position (especially at pantomime time) to flutter the country theatrical dove-cot; repeated "last appearances" are not absolutely things of a bye-gone day; "literary gentlemen" are now and then known to purloin plots; and the great question concerning newspaper paragraphs, which Mr. Crummles summed up in the words, "I can't think who puts these things in. *I* didn't," remains unanswered.

With all their little foibles the Crummles company were a genial, merry, honest set of people. One reads of them with delight, and takes leave of them with regret. They may not, from the severely critical point of view, have been a credit to the stage; but who can say that they disgraced it?

In "Martin Chuzzlewit," brief mention of the stage is made in a manner far less agreeable. At the house of the fashionable Mr. Tigg Montague, Jonas Chuzzlewit was presented to a certain Mr. Pip, with the recommendation that he was a "theatrical man—capital man to know—oh, capital man!" and in the course of the conversation, this engaging gentleman told the following dainty anecdote:

"'But the Viscount's the boy,' cried Pip, who invented a new oath for the introduction of everything he said. 'The Viscount's the boy! He came into our place one night to take Her home, rather slued, but not much, and said, "Where's Pip? I want to see Pip. Produce Pip!" "What is the row, my lord?" "Shakespeare's an infernal humbug, Pip! What's the good of Shakespeare, Pip? I never read him. What the devil is it all about, Pip? There's a lot of feet in Shakespeare's verse, but there ain't legs worth mentioning in Shakespeare's plays, are there, Pip? Juliet, Desdemona, Lady Macbeth, and all the rest of 'em, whatever their names are, might as well have no legs at all, for anything the audience know about it, Pip. Why, in that respect they're all Miss Biffins to the audience, Pip. I'll tell you what it is. What the people call dramatic poetry is a collection of sermons. Do I go to the theatre to be lectured? No, Pip.

If I wanted that, I'd go to church. What is the legitimate object of the drama, Pip? Human nature. What are legs? Human nature. Then let us have plenty of leg pieces, Pip, and I'll stand by you, my buck!" 'And I am proud to say,' added Pip, 'that he *did* stand by me, handsomely!'"

If it can be said of him that he really belonged to the stage, Mr. Pip certainly disgraced it.

In "Dombey and Son," and "David Copperfield," although it should not be forgotten that David in his salad days saw "Julius Cæsar" performed at Covent Garden, and thought that "to have all those Roman nobles alive before me, and walking in and out for my entertainment, instead of being the stern task-masters they had been at school, was a most novel and delightful effect," there is little or no mention made of the theatre, or of theatrical people; and a few years ago the same might have been said of "Bleak House," but now that the concert-hall furnishes so many recruits to the stage, a little space in these pages surely need not be grudged to the famous "Little Swills."

"Bleak House" was written long before the days when the palatial concert-halls of the present time had sprung into existence, and "Little Swills," who might nowadays have been driving his own well-appointed carriage, and doing three or four highly remunerative "turns" nightly, was perforce obliged to exercise his talent in the first-floor room at the "Sol's Arms," hard by Chancery Lane, where harmonic meetings took place twice weekly, and where a window-bill expressed a hope that his (Little Swills's) friends would "rally round him and support first-rate talent." Little Swills, who is described as "a chubby little man, with a moist eye and an inflamed nose," was of a persevering disposition, and was evidently great at "topical allusions," for did he not make a point of being present at the inquest held at the Sol's Arms on the body of the unhappy law writer, with a view of getting up an imitation of the coroner, and making it a principal feature of the harmonic meeting in the evening?—and did he not redeem his intention by saying at that intellectual and convivial gathering, "Gentlemen, if you'll permit me, I'll attempt a short description of a scene of real life that came off here to-day"? Whereupon, being much applauded and encouraged, he went out of the room as Swills, came in as the coroner ("not the least in the world like him"), described the inquest, with recreative intervals of pianoforte accompaniment to the refrain, "With his (the coroner's) tippy tol li doll, tippy tol lo doll, tippy tol li doll, Dee!" In the hot summer months the harmonic meetings at the "Sol's Arms," were discontinued, and then Little Swills was engaged at the Pastoral Gardens down the river, "where he comes out in quite an innocent manner, and sings comic ditties of a juvenile complexion, calculated (as the bill says) not to wound the feelings of the most fastidious mind"; but on the night of the terrible death of old Krook, he was back in his old quarters, and "after keeping the lovers of harmony in a roar like a very Yorick," was heard " taking the gruff line in a concerted piece, and sentimentally adjuring his friends and patrons to 'Listen, listen, listen, Tew the wa-ter Fall!'" and, later on, when the Smallweed family had taken mysterious possession of the Krook establishment, he was to the fore with " what are professionally known as 'patter' allusions to the subject"; his efforts being well-seconded by those of Miss M. Melvilleson "in the revived Caledonian melody of ' We're a' nodding,'" that eminent vocalist pointing the sentiment that "'the dogs love broo' (whatever the nature of that refreshment may be) with such archness and such a turn of the head towards next door, that she is immediately understood to mean Mr. Smallweed loves to find money, and is nightly honcured with a double encore."

And so Mr. Swills passes out of the glorious pages of "Bleak House," and the reader is left in wonder whether he ever became accepted on the Stage proper as one of the leading comedians of the day. Perhaps, however, poor Little Swills flourished before his time, and in the degenerate days when comedy, or even comic acting, was preferred to concert-hall singing.

In "Little Dorrit" there is a very touching description of poor old Frederick Dorrit in the days when he played the clarionet in a small London theatre, and a very graphic description of a ballet rehearsal which took place on the day when Little Dorrit herself, in her anxiety concerning her flighty sister Fanny, found her way into the mysterious world "behind the scenes."

"Little Dorrit was almost as ignorant of the ways of theatres as of the ways of gold mines, and when she was directed to a furtive sort of door, with a curious up-all-night air about it, that appeared to be ashamed of itself and to be hiding in an alley, she hesitated to approach it, being further deterred by the sight of some half-dozen close-shaved gentlemen, with their hats very strangely on, who were hanging about the door, looking not at all unlike Collegians. On her applying to them, reassured by this resemblance, for a direction to Miss Dorrit, they made way for her to enter a dark hall—it was more like a great grim lamp gone out than anything else—where she could hear the distant playing of music and the sound of dancing feet. A man so much in want of airing that he had a blue mould upon him, sat watching this dark place from a hole in a corner, like a spider; and he told her that he would send a message up to Miss Dorrit by the first lady or gentleman that went through. The first lady who went through had a roll of music, half in her muff and half out of it, and was in such a tumbled condition altogether that it seemed as if it would be an act of kindness to iron her. But as she was very good-natured, and said 'Come with me; I'll soon find Miss Dorrit for you,' Miss Dorrit's sister went with her, drawing nearer and nearer at every step she took in the darkness to the sound of music and the sound of dancing feet."

"At last they came into a maze of dust, where a quantity of people were tumbling over one another, and where there was such a confusion of unaccountable shapes and beams, bulkheads, brick walls, ropes and rollers, and such a mixing of gaslight and daylight, that they seemed to have got on the wrong side of the pattern of the universe. Little Dorrit, left to herself, and knocked against by somebody every minute, was quite bewildered when she heard her sister's voice."

The conversation between the sisters requires no record here, and indeed, it was very soon interrupted, as was also the chattering of a number of young ladies who sat on anything they could find, who all " wanted ironing," and who all " had a curious way of looking everywhere while they chattered," by " a monotonous boy in a Scotch cap," who put his head round a beam on the left, and said, " Less noise there, ladies ! " and by " a sprightly gentleman, with a quantity of black hair," who put his head round a beam on the right, and said, " Less noise there, darlings."

This couple having very shortly afterwards severally given the warning of " Look out there, ladies," and " Look out there, darlings," all " the young ladies rose, and began shaking their skirts out behind," and when " Now ladies," and " Now darlings," had been cried, Little Dorrit was left alone to listen to the music and the dancing feet, and the accompaniment of the voice of the gentleman with the black hair, who was continually calling out, ' " One, two, three, four, five, six—go ! One, two, three, four, five, six—go ! Steady, darlings ! One, two, three, four, five, six—go ! ' " Ultimately the voice stopped, and they all came back again, more or less out of breath, folding themselves in their shawls, and making ready for the streets, and when the boy and the man had in their accustomed manner, and each from his own beam, said, " Everybody at eleven to-morrow, ladies," and

"Everybody at eleven to-morrow, darlings," Amy and Fanny Dorrit were left to themselves.

"When they were alone, something was rolled up or by other means got out of the way, and there was a great empty well before them, looking down into the depths of which, Fanny said, 'Now Uncle!' Little Dorrit, as her eyes became used to the darkness, faintly made him out, at the bottom of the well, in an obscure corner by himself, with his instrument in its ragged case under his arm."

"The old man looked as if the remote high gallery windows, with their little strip of sky, might have been the point of his better fortunes, from which he had descended until he had gradually sunk down below there to the bottom. He had been in that place six nights a week for many years, but had never been observed to raise his eyes above his music-book, and was confidently believed to have never seen a play. There were legends in the place that he did not so much as know the popular heroes and heroines by sight, and that the low comedian had 'mugged' at him in his richest manner fifty nights for a wager, and he had shown no trace of consciousness. The carpenters had a joke that he was dead without being aware of it, and the frequenters of the pit supposed him to pass his whole life, night and day, and Sunday and all, in the orchestra. They had tried him a few times with pinches of snuff offered over the rails, and he had always responded to this attention with a momentary waking-up of manner that had the pale phantom of a gentleman in it; beyond this he never, on any occasion, had any other part in what was going on than the part written out for the clarionet: in private life, where there was no part for the clarionet, he had no part at all."

In this there is something so terribly pathetic that it is almost a relief to know that in " Great Expectations," Dickens returned to his earlier and humorous view of theatrical life.

From the moment when the appreciative reader is introduced to the pompous, Roman-nosed, parish clerk, Mr. Wopsle, who was convinced that if the Church was " thrown open," he would speedily make his mark in it, he finds himself in the best of good company, and when Mr. Wopsle changes his name to Waldengarver, and tries his fortune on the stage, he is seen at his greatest; albeit Joe Gargery expressed it as his opinion that in his change of life he had " had a drop."

"'Had a drop, Joe?' enquired Pip.

"' Why, yes,' said Joe, lowering his voice, ' he's left the Church and went into the play-acting.

Which the play-acting have likeways brought him to London along with me. And his wish were, if no offence, as I would 'and you that.'

Pip took what Joe gave him, and found it to be "the crumpled play-bill of a small metropolitan theatre, announcing the first appearance in that very week of 'the celebrated Provincial Amateur of Roscian renown, whose unique performances in the highest tragic walk of our National Bard has lately occasioned so great a sensation in local dramatic circles.'

"'Were you at his performance, Joe?' inquired Pip.

"'I *were*,' said Joe, with emphasis and solemnity.

"'Was there a great sensation?'

"'Why,' said Joe, 'yes, there certainly were a peck of orange-peel. Partickler when he see the ghost. Though I put it to yourself, sir, whether it were calc'lated to keep a man up to his work with a good heart, to be continually cutting in betwixt him and the ghost with "Amen!" A man may have had a misfortun' and been in the Church, but that is no reason why you should put him out at such a time. Which I meanter say, if the ghost of a man's own father cannot be allowed to claim his attention, what can, sir? Still more, when his mourning 'at is unfortunately made so small as that the weight of the black feathers brings it off, try to keep it on how you may.'"

Pip's experience of Mr. Wopsle's (or Mr. Waldengarver's) performance of Hamlet, is described by him as follows :—

"On our arrival in Denmark, we found the king and queen of that country elevated in two arm-chairs, on a kitchen table, holding a Court. The whole of the Danish nobility were in attendance; consisting of a noble boy, in the wash-leather boots of a gigantic ancestor, a venerable peer with a dirty face, who seemed to have risen from the people late in life, and the Danish chivalry with a comb in its hair and a pair of white silk legs, and presenting on the whole a feminine appearance. My gifted townsman stood gloomily apart, with folded arms, and I could have wished that his curls and forehead had been more probable.

"Several curious little circumstances transpired as the action proceeded. The late king of the country not only appeared to have been troubled with a cough at the time of his decease, but to have taken it with him to the tomb, and to have brought it back. The royal phantom also carried a ghostly manuscript round its truncheon, to which it had the appearance of occasionally referring, and that, too, with an air of anxiety and a tendency to lose the place of reference which were suggestive of a state of mortality. It was this, I conceive, which led to the shade's being advised by the gallery to 'turn over!'—a recommendation which it took extremely ill. It was likewise to be noted of this majestic spirit that whereas it always appeared with an air of having been out a long time and walked an immense distance, it perceptibly came from a closely contiguous wall. This occasioned its terrors to be received derisively. The Queen of Denmark, a very buxom lady, though no doubt historically brazen, was considered by the public to have too much brass about her; her chin being attached to her diadem by a broad band of that metal (as if she had gorgeous toothache), her waist being encircled by another, and each of her arms by another, so that she was openly mentioned as the 'kettledrum.'

" The noble boy in the ancestral boots, was inconsistent, representing himself, as it were in one breath, as an able seaman, a strolling actor, a gravedigger, a clergyman, and a person of the utmost importance at a Court fencing match, on the authority of whose practised eye and nice discrimination the finest strokes were judged. This gradually led to a want of toleration for him, and even—on his being detected in holy orders and declining to perform the funeral service —to the general indignation taking the form of nuts. Lastly, Ophelia was a prey to such slow musical madness, that when, in course of time, she had taken off her white muslin scarf, folded it up, and buried it, a sulky man who had been cooling his impatient nose against an iron bar in the front row of the gallery, growled, 'Now the baby's put to bed let's have supper!' Which, to say the least of it, was out of keeping.

"Upon my unfortunate townsman all these incidents accumulated with playful effect. Whenever that undecided Prince had to ask a question or state a doubt, the public helped him out with it. As for example, on the question whether it was nobler in the mind to suffer, some roared yes, and some no, and some inclining to both opinions said 'toss up for it," and quite a Debating Society arose. When he asked what such fellows as he do crawling between earth and heaven, he was encouraged with loud cries of 'Hear, hear!' When he appeared with his stocking disordered (its disorder expressed, according to usage, by one very neat fold in the top, which I suppose always to be got up with a flat iron), a conversation took place in the gallery respecting the paleness of his leg, and whether it was occasioned by the turn the ghost had given him. On his taking the recorders—very like a little black flute that had just been played in the orchestra and handed out at the door—he was called upon unanimously for

Rule Britannia. When he recommended the player not to saw the air thus, the sulky man said, 'And don't you do it neither; you're a deal worse than *him!*' And I grieve to say that peals of laughter greeted Mr. Wopsle on every one of these occasions.

"But his greatest trials were in the churchyard, which had the appearance of a primeval forest, with a kind of small ecclesiastical washhouse on one side, and a turnpike gate on the other. Mr. Wopsle in a comprehensive black cloak, being descried entering at the turnpike, the gravedigger was admonished in a friendly way, 'Look out! There's the undertaker a coming, to see how you're getting on with your work!' I believe it is well known in a constitutional country that Mr. Wopsle could not possibly have returned the skull, after moralising over it, without dusting his fingers on a white napkin taken from his breast; but even that innocent and indispensable action did not pass without the comment 'Wai-ter!' The arrival of the body for interment (in an empty black box with the lid tumbling open) was the signal for a general joy which was much enhanced by the discovery, among the bearers of an individual obnoxious to identification. The joy attended Mr. Wopsle through his struggle with Laertes on the brink of the orchestra and the grave, and slackened no more until he had tumbled the King off the kitchen-table, and had died by inches from the ankles upwards."

Those who have been present at a theatrical entertainment when an unholy "joy" of this kind inspires an irreverently disposed gallery will always keenly relish the truth and the rich humour of this inimitable description; and those who have had any experience of the absolutely incurable conceit of the amateur actor who believes himself capable of impersonating exacting characters, which, after life-long study, are rarely perfect in the hands of the professional player, will not feel the least atom of surprise on finding that even after this merciless "guying," Mr. Wopsle—or, "Mr. Waldengarver"—was self-satisfied, sanguine, and serene.

"'How did you like my reading of the character, gentlemen?' said Mr. Waldengarver, almost, if not quite, with patronage on the subsequent visit of Pip and Herbert Pocket to his dressing-room.

" Herbert said from behind (again poking me), ' massive and concrete.' So I said boldly, as if I had originated it, and must beg to insist upon it, 'massive and concrete.'

"' I am glad to have your approbation, gentlemen,' said Mr. Waldengarver, with dignity.

"'But I'll tell you one thing, Mr. Waldengarver,' said the 'dresser,' who was divesting him of his Danish garments, 'in which you're out in your reading. Now mind! I don't care who says the contrary; I tell you so. You're out in your reading of Hamlet when you get your legs in profile. The last Hamlet as I dressed, made the same mistakes in his reading at rehearsal, till I got him to put a large red wafer on each of his shins, and then at that rehearsal (which was the last) I went in front, sir, to the back of the pit, and whenever his reading brought him into profile, I called out, "I don't see no wafers!" And at night his reading was lovely.'

"Mr. Waldengarver smiled at me, as much as to say 'a faithful dependent—I overlook his folly;' and then said aloud, 'My view is a little classic and thoughful for them here; but they will improve, they will improve.'

"'Did you observe gentlemen,' continued Mr. Waldengarver, 'that there was a man in the gallery who endeavoured to cast derision on the service—I mean the representation?'

"We basely replied that we rather thought we had noticed such a man. I added, 'He was drunk, no doubt.'

"'Oh dear no, sir,' said Mr. Wopsle, 'not drunk. His employer would see to that sir. His employer would not allow him to be drunk.'

"'You know his employer?' said I.

"Mr. Wopsle shut his eyes, and opened them again, performing both ceremonies very slowly.

"'You must have observed gentlemen,' said he, 'an ignorant and blatant ass, with a rasping throat, and a countenance expressive of low malignity, who went through—I will not say sustained—the rôle (if I may use a French expression) of Claudius, King of Denmark. That is his employer, gentlemen. Such is the profession.'"

Pip is charitable enough to say that he did not know "whether he should have been more sorry for Mr. Wopsle if he had been in despair." but Dickens, no doubt, knew that men of the Wopsle class (and there are plenty of them) require no pity, but are, on the contrary, to be envied for their impenetrable and always self-sustaining vanity.

Mr. Wopsle, however, did not rise to fame by leaps and bounds, for on the next occasion when Pip visited the theatre which was fortunate enough to claim him as a member of its company, he found—"A virtuous boatswain in his Majesty's service—a most excellent man, though I could have wished his trousers not quite so tight in some places and not quite so loose in others—who knocked all the little men's hats over their eyes, though he was very generous and brave, and who would'nt hear of anybody paying taxes, though he was very patriotic. He had a bag of money in his pocket, like a pudding in the cloth, and on that property married a young person in bed furniture, with great rejoicings; the whole population of Portsmouth (nine in number at the last census) turning out on the beach, to rub their own hands and shake everybody else's, and sing 'fill, fill!' A certain dark-complexioned Swab, however, who wouldn't fill or do anything else that was proposed to him, and whose heart was openly stated (by the boatswain) to be as black as his figure-head, proposed to two other Swabs to get all mankind into difficulties; which was so effectually done (the Swab family having considerable political influence) that it took half the evening to get things right, and then it was only brought about through an honest little grocer, with a white hat, black gaiters and red nose, getting into a clock with a gridiron, and listening, and coming out, and knocking everybody down from behind with the gridiron whom he couldn't confute with what he had overheard. This led to Mr. Wopsle's (who had never been heard of before) coming in with a star and garter on, as a plenipotentiary of great power, direct from the Admiralty, to say that the Swabs were all to go to prison on the spot, and that he had brought the boatswain down the Union Jack, as a slight acknowledg- of his public services. The boatswain, unmanned for the first time, respectfully dried his eyes on the Jack, and then cheering up and addressing Mr. Wopsle as Your Honour, solicited permission to take him by the fin. Mr. Wopsle conceding his fin with a gracious dignity, was immediately shoved into a dusty corner while everybody danced a hornpipe, and from that corner, surveying the public with a discontented eye, became aware of me.

"The second piece was the last new grand comic Christmas pantomime, in the first scene of which it pained me to suspect that I detected Mr. Wopsle with red worsted legs, under a highly magnified phosphoric countenance, and a shock of red curtain fringe for his hair, engaged in the manufacture of thunderbolts in a mine, and displaying great cowardice when his gigantic master came home (very hoarse) to dinner. But he presently presented himself under worthier circumstances, for the Genius of Youthful Love being in want of assistance—on account of the parental brutality of an ignorant farmer, who opposed the choice of his daughter's heart by purposely falling upon the object in a flour-sack, out of the first-floor window—summoned a sententious enchanter, and he, coming up from the antipodes rather unsteadily, after an apparently violent journey, proved to be Mr. Wopsle, in a high-crowned hat, with a necromantic work in one volume under his arm. The business of this enchanter on earth being principally to be talked at, sung at, butted at, danced at, and flashed at with fires of various colours, he had a good deal of time on his hands."

Very incomplete would be this portion of the writer's task without due mention being made of the "P. Salcy Family," whose names figure in that chapter of "The Uncommercial Traveller," entitled "In the French Flemish Country." Finding himself in this locality, and deciding to stay there, Dickens says :—

"What part in my decision was borne by Monsieur P. Salcy is of no moment, though I own to encountering that gentleman's name on a red bill on the wall before I made up my mind. Monsieur P. Salcy, '*par permission de M. le Maire,*' had established his theatre in the whitewashed Hotel de Ville, on the steps of which illustrious edifice I stood. And Monsieur P. Salcy, privileged director of such theatre, situate in 'the first theatrical arrondissement of the department of the North,' invited French-Flemish mankind to come and partake of the intellectual banquet provided by his family of dramatic artists, fifteen subjects in number.

'*La Famille P. Salcy, composée d'artistes dramatiques, au nombre de 15 sujets.*'

*   *   *   *   *   *

"The members of the Family P. Salcy were so fat and so like one another, fathers, mothers, sisters, brothers, uncles and aunts, that I think the local audience were much confused about the plot of the piece under representation, and to the last expected that everybody must turn out to be the long-lost relative of everybody else. The theatre was established on the top storey of the Hotel de Ville, and was approached by a long bare staircase, whereon, in an airy situation, one of the P. Salcy Family—a stout gentleman, imperfectly repressed by a belt—took the money. This occasioned the greatest excitement of the evening, for, no sooner did the curtain rise on the introductory vaudeville, and reveal in the person of the young lover (singing a very short song with his eyebrows) apparently the very same identical stout gentleman imperfectly repressed by a belt, than everybody rushed out to the paying place, to ascertain if he could possibly have put on that dress-coat, that clear complexion, and those arched black vocal eyebrows, in so short a space of time. It then became manifest that this was another stout gentleman, imperfectly repressed by a belt, to whom, before the spectators had recovered their presence of mind, entered a third stout gentleman, imperfectly repressed by a belt, exactly like him. These two 'subjects,' making, with the money-taker, three of the announced fifteen, fell into conversation touching a charming young widow, who, presently appearing, proved to be a stout lady, altogether irrepressible by any means—quite a parallel case to the American negro—fourth of the fifteen subjects and sister of the fifth, who presided over the check department. In good time the whole of the fifteen subjects were dramatically presented, and we had the inevitable *Ma Mère, Ma Mère*, and also the inevitable *malédiction d'un père*, and likewise the inevitable Marquis, and also the inevitable provincial young man, weak-minded but faithful, who followed Julie to Paris, and cried and laughed and choked all at once. The story was brought out with the help of a virtuous spinning wheel in the beginning, a vicious set of diamonds in the middle, and a rheumatic blessing (which arrived by post), from Ma Mére towards the end; the whole resulting in a small sword in the body of one of the stout gentlemen, imperfectly repressed by a belt, fifty thousand francs per annum, and a decoration to the other stout gentleman, imperfectly repressed by a belt, and an assurance from everybody to the provincial young man that if he were not supremely happy—which he seemed to have no reason whatever for being—he ought to be. This afforded him a fine opportunity for crying and laughing and choking all at once, and sent the audience home sentimentally delighted. Audience more attentive or better behaved there could not possibly be, though the places in the second rank in the theatre of the Family P. Salcy were sixpence each in English money, and the places of first rank a shilling. How the fifteen subjects ever got so fat upon it, the kind Heavens know."

This delightful description of a common-place French play, in the hands of a common-place French company—though, by the way, the dismal "Ma Mère, Ma Mère" refrain is not unknown even within the classic walls of the Théâtre Français—is preceded in the pages of "The Uncommercial Traveller" by a theatrical chapter, entitled "Two Views of a Cheap Theatre." In it Dickens says: "I walked up Bow Street, disposed to be angry with the shops there that were letting out theatrical secrets by exhibiting to work-a-day humanity the stuff of which diadems and robes of kings are made. I noticed that some shops which had once been in the dramatic line, and had struggled out of it, were not getting on prosperously—like some actors I have known, who took to business and failed to make it answer.

In a word, those streets looked so dull, and, considered as theatrical streets, so broken and bankrupt, that the 'FOUND DEAD' on the blackboard at the police-station might have announced the decease of the Drama, and the pools of water outside the fire-engine makers at the corner of Long Acre might have been occasioned by his having brought out the whole of his stock to play upon its last smouldering ashes.

"And yet, on such a night, in so degenerate a time, the object of my journey was theatrical. And yet, within half an hour, I was in an immense theatre, capable of holding nearly five thousand people.

"What theatre? Her Majesty's? Far better Royal Italian Opera? Far better. Infinitely superior to the latter for hearing in; infinitely superior to both for seeing in. To every part of this theatre, spacious fire-proof ways of ingress and egress. For every part of it, convenient places of refreshment and retiring rooms. Everything to eat and drink carefully supervised as to quality, and sold at an appointed price; respectable female attendants ready for the commonest women in the audience; a general air of consideration, decorum, and supervision, most commendable; an unquestionably humanising influence in all the social arrangements of the place.

"Surely a dear theatre, then? Because there

were in London (not very long ago) theatres with entrance-prices up to half-a-guinea a head, whose arrangements were not half so civilised. Surely, therefore, a dear theatre? Not very dear. A gallery at threepence, another gallery at fourpence, a pit at sixpence, boxes and pit-stalls at a shilling, and a few private boxes at half-a-crown.

"My uncommercial curiosity induced me to go into every nook of this great place, and among every class of the audience assembled in it— amounting that evening, as I calculated, to about two thousand and odd hundreds. Magnificently lighted by a firmament of sparkling chandeliers, the building was ventilated to perfection. My sense of smell, without being particularly delicate, has been so offended in some of the commoner places of public resort, that I have often been obliged to leave them when I have made an uncommercial journey expressly to look on. The air of this theatre was fresh, cool, and wholesome. To help towards this end, very sensible precautions had been used, ingeniously combining the experience of hospitals and railway stations. Asphalt pavement substituted for wooden floors, honest bare walls of glazed brick and tile—even at the back of the boxes—for plaster and paper, no benches stuffed, and no carpeting or baize used; a cool material with a light glazed surface, being the covering of the seats.

"These various contrivances are as well considered in the place in question as if it were a Fever Hospital; the result is that it is sweet and healthful. It has been constructed, from the ground to the roof, with a careful reference to sight and sound in every corner; the result is, that its form is beautiful, and that the appearance of the audience, as seen from the proscenium—with every face in it commanding the stage, and the whole so admirably raked and turned to that centre, that a hand can scarcely move in the great assemblage without the movement being seen from thence—is highly remarkable in its union of vastness with compactness. The stage itself, and all its appurtenances of machinery, cellarage, height and breadth, are on a scale more like the Scala at Milan, or the San Carlo at Naples, or the Grand Opera at Paris, than any notion a stranger would be likely to form of the Britannia Theatre at Hoxton, a mile north of St. Luke's Hospital, in the Old Street Road, London. The 'Forty Thieves' might be played here, and every thief ride his real horse, and the disguised captain bring in his oil jars on a train of real camels, and nobody be put out of the way. This really extraordinary place is the achievement of one man's enterprise, and was erected on the ruins of an inconvenient old building in less than five months, at a round cost of five-and-twenty thousand pounds. To dismiss this part of my subject, and still to render to the proprietor the credit that is strictly his due, I must add that his sense of the responsibility upon him to make the best of his audience, and to do his best for them, is a highly agreeable sign of these times."

It is pleasant to know that what is here said of the great East-end playhouse that thus aroused the admiration of Dickens may with equal truth be said to-day. ' Under the experienced and admirable management of Mrs. Sarah Lane, the Britannia Theatre, Hoxton—or the " Brit," as it is affectionately termed by its frequenters—is a most popular, prosperous, and well-conducted place of theatrical entertainment. The house, too, can claim for itself the distinction of being the only one that produces Christmas pantomimes founded upon other lines than those of the worn out themes which continually do duty at other theatres all England over.

It was a pantomime that Dickens saw on the occasion of his visit, and which, in his own inimitable way, he thus sums up :—

" We began at half-past six with a pantomime —with a pantomime so long, that before it was over I felt as if I had been travelling for six weeks—going to India, say, by the Overland Mail. The Spirit of Liberty was the principal personage in the Introduction, and the Four Quarters of the World came out of the globe, glittering, and discoursed with the Spirit, who sang charmingly. We were delighted to understand that there was no liberty anywhere but among ourselves, and we highly applauded the agreeable fact. In an allegorical way, which did as well as any other way, we and the Spirit of Liberty got into a Kingdom of Needles and Pins, and found them at war with a potentate who called in to his aid their old arch-enemy Rust, and who would have got the better of them if the Spirit of Liberty had not in the nick of time transformed the leaders into Clown, Pantaloon, Harlequin, Columbine, Harlequina, and a whole family of Sprites, consisting of a remarkably stout father and three spineless sons. We all knew what was coming when the Spirit of Liberty addressed the King with the big face, and His Majesty backed to the side-scenes and began untying himself behind with his big face all on one side. Our excitement at that crisis was great, and our delight unbounded. After this era in our existence, we went through all the incidents of a pantomime; it was not by any means a savage pantomime, in the way of burning or boiling people, or throwing them out of window, or cutting them up; was often very roll; was always liberally got up, and cleverly presented. I noticed that the people who kept the shops, and who represented the passengers in the thoroughfares, and so forth, had no conventionality in them, but were unusually like the real thing—from which I infer that you may take that audience in (if you wish to) concerning Knights and Ladies, Fairies, Angels, or such like, but they are not to be done as to anything in the streets. I noticed, also, that when two young men, dressed in exact imitation of the eel-and-sausage-cravated portion of the audience, were chased by policemen, and, finding themselves in danger of being caught, dropped so suddenly as to oblige the policemen to tumble over them, there was great rejoicing—as though it were a delicate reference to something they had heard of before."

"The pantomime was succeeded by a Melc-Drama. Throughout the evening I was pleased to observe Virtue quite as triumphant as she usually is out of doors, and indeed I thought rather more so. We all agreed (for the time) that honesty was the best policy, and we were as hard as iron upon Vice, and we wouldn't hear of Villainy getting on in the world—no, not on any consideration whatever."

"Between the pieces, we almost all of us went out and refreshed. Many of us went the length of drinking beer at the bars of the neighbouring public-houses, some of us drank spirits, crowds of us had sandwiches and ginger-beer at the refreshment bars established for us in the theatre. The sandwich—as substantial as was consistent with portability, and as cheap as possible—we hailed as one of our greatest institutions. It forced its way among us at all stages of the entertainment, and we were always delighted to see it; its adaptability to the varying moods of our nature was surprising; we could never weep so comfortably as when our tears fell on our sandwich; we could never laugh so heartily as when we choked with sandwich; Virtue never looked so beautiful, or Vice so deformed as when we paused, sandwich in hand, to consider what would come of that resolution of Wickedness in boots to sever Innocence in flowered chintz from Honest Industry in striped stockings. When the curtain fell for the night, we still fell back upon sandwich, to help us through the rain and mud, and home to bed."

The second half of this eminently theatrical chapter deals with a Sunday religious service held in the same theatre—in connection with which Dickens pointedly notes that "the lowest part of the audience of the previous night *was not there*." Concerning such services he says: "That these Sunday meetings in theatres are good things I do not doubt. Nor do I doubt that they will work lower and lower down in the social scale, if those who preside over them will be very careful on two heads; firstly, not to disparage the places in which they speak, or the intelligence of their hearers; secondly, not to set themselves in antagonism to the natural inborn desire of the mass of mankind to recreate themselves and to be amused."

Stronger testimony than this of the estimation in which Dickens held the stage, could hardly be advanced.

Unless mention be made of the little French actress, who, whimsically described as "The Compact Enchantress," is one of his fellow travellers on that wonderfully described journey from London Bridge to Paris, to be found in that chapter of the "Reprinted Pieces," entitled "A Flight," and to whom he says, "I yielded up my heart under the auspices of that brave child, MEAT-CHELL, at the St. James's Theatre the night before last," reference to the theatrical characters and scenes to be found in the published works of Dickens is now practically exhausted—but stay, the clown is still a sort of connecting link between the stage and the circus, and no one will grudge a word in these pages to "Sleary's Horsemanship," the humorous account of which enlivens the somewhat gloomy chapters of "Hard Times," especially as the lisping words of its warm-hearted old proprietor seem very well to sum up all that Dickens felt in writing of things connected with the theatre.

"People mutht be amuthed," said Mr. Sleary to Mr. Gradgrind, "they can't be alwayth a learning, nor yet they can't be alwayth a working, they ain't made for it. You *mutht* have uth, Thquire. Do the withe thing and the kind thing, too, and make the betht of uth, not the wurtht."

This is exactly what Dickens did. It is a little curious, perhaps, to note, that in all his allusions to the stage he chose its comic and even sometimes its seamy side; but that he was an enthusiastic admirer of, and a firm believer in it, in its better and intellectual phases, the later portions of this book will amply show.

CHAPTER III.

DICKENS AS A DRAMATIST.

In that pleasant "series of daily companions," happily entitled "The best of all Good Company," Mr. Blanchard Jerrold in his "Day with Charles Dickens," after bearing testimony to his intense love for the stage, the excellence of his acting, and the high opinion that Douglas Jerrold had of his dramatic judgment, gives the following letter addressed to the author of "Time Works Wonders," and "Black Eye'd Susan."

"Devonshire Terrace,
"Thirteenth June, 1843.

"My Dear Jerrold,—Yes, you have anticipated my occupation. Chuzzlewit be hanged—high comedy and five hundred pounds are the only matters I can think of. I call it 'The One Thing Needful; or, the Part is Better than the Whole.' Here are the characters:—

Old Febrile . . .	Mr. Farren.
Young Febrile *(his son)* .	Mr. Howe.
Jack Hessians *(his friend)* .	Mr. W. Lacy.

Chalks (*a landlord*)	Mr. Gough.
Hon. Harry Staggers	Mr. Mellon.
Sir Thomas Tip	Mr. Buckstone.
Swig	Mr. Webster.
The Duke of Leeds	Mr. Coutts.
Sir Smiven Growler	Mr. Macready.

Servants, gamblers, visitors, etc.

Mrs. Febrile	Mrs. Glover.
Lady Tip	Mrs. Humby.
Mrs. Sour	Mrs. Clifford.
Fanny	Miss A. Smith.

"One scene, where old Febrile tickles Lady Tip in the ribs, and afterwards dances out with his hat behind him, his stick before, and his eye on the pit, I expect will bring the house down. There is also another point—where old Febrile, at the conclusion of his disclosure to Swig, rises and says, 'And now, Mr. Swig, tell me, have I acted well?' and Swig says, 'Well, Mr. Febrile, have you ever acted ill?' which will carry off the piece."

Dashed off in high spirits in a letter to an appreciative friend how admirably are the old names, and the old humours of the comedy of a bye-gone day here travestied! What could not Dickens have done in the regions of extravaganza and burlesque?

In the same letter, after dealing with other matters, he goes on to say:—

"But I have my comedy to fly to—my only comfort! I walk up and down the street at the back of the theatre every night, and peep in at the green-room window, thinking of the time when 'Dick-ens' will be called for by excited hundreds, and won't come—till Mr. Webster (half-Swig-and-half-himself) shall enter from his dressing-room, and quelling the tempest with a smile, beseech that wizard if he be in the house (here he looks up at my box), to accept the congratulations of the audience and indulge them with a sight of the man who had got five hundred pounds in money, and it's imposible to say how much in laurels. Then I shall come forward and bow, once, twice, thrice—roars of approbation. Bravyo! brarvo'! Hooray! hoorar! hooroar!—one cheer more—and asking Webster home to supper, shall declare eternal friendship for that public-spirited individual, which Talfourd (the vice) will echo with all his heart and soul, and with tears in his eyes, adding in a perfectly audible voice, and in the same breath, that " he's a very wretched cweature, but better than Macweady any way, for he wouldn't play Ion when it was given to him.' After which he will propose said Macready's health in terms of red-hot eloquency."

"I am always, my dear Jerrold, faithfully your friend,

"THE CONGREVE OF THE 19TH CENTURY

("Which I mean to be called in the Sunday papers.)

"P.S.—I shall dedicate it to Webster, beginning:—

"'MY DEAR SIR,—When you first proposed to stimulate the slumbering dramatic talent of England, I assure you I had not the least idea, etc., etc., etc.'"

Alas, the comedy of his whimsical imagination was never written, and his name as a dramatist is chiefly associated with the three trivial pieces mentioned in the introductory chapter, and which, nowadays, are only interesting and valuable to the increasing number of collectors of "Dickensiana." The libretto of "The Village Coquettes," which was in 1837 sold for tenpence, is now worth two guineas. "The Strange Gentleman," and "Is She His Wife? or, Something Singular," are exceedingly precious, and playbills of each will realise a guinea.

Of some of these, the following are copies:—

ST. JAMES'S  THEATRE.

Never Acted !

This Evening, Tuesday, December 6th, 1836,

Will be performed (FIRST TIME) an entirely new Operatic Burletta, with New and Beautiful Scenery, appropriate Dresses and Decorations, to be called

THE VILLAGE COQUETTES.

The Drama and Words of the Songs by "Boz." The music by John Hullah.

SCENE—An English Village.   PERIOD—The Autumn of 1729.

Squire Norton	Mr. Braham.
The Honorable Sparkins Flam (*his friend*) .	Mr. M. Barnett.
Old Benson (*a small farmer*)	Mr. Strickland.
Mr. Martin Stokes (*a very small farmer with a very large circle of particular friends*)	Mr. Harley.
George Edmunds (*betrothed to Lucy*) . .	Mr. Bennett.
Young Benson	Mr. John Parry.
John Maddox (*attached to Rose*) . . .	Mr. Gardner.
Lucy Benson	Miss Rainforth.
Rose (*her cousin*)	Miss Julia Smith.

Villagers, Gamekeepers, Servants, Domestics, by the rest of the Company, assisted by a numerous train of Auxiliaries.

Incidental to the Burletta the following Pieces of Music:

OVERTURE.

ACT I.

ROUND AND CHORUS.	"Hail to the Merry Autumn Days."
SONG.—Miss Rainforth.	"Love is not a feeling to pass away."
SONG.—Mr. Braham, and Chorus.	"The Cares of the Day."
SONG.—Mr. Bennett.	"Autumn Leaves."
SONG.—Miss Julia Smith.	"Some folks who have grown old and sour."
DUET.—Miss Julia Smith and Mr. M. Barnett.	"Mr. Flam and his beautiful Rose."
SCENE.—Mr. Braham.	"The Child and the Old Man."
DUET.—Miss Rainforth and Mr. Braham.	"In Rich and Lofty Stations Shine."
FINALE TO THE FIRST ACT.	"Turn him from his Farm." All the Principals and Chorus.

6*

ACT II.

QUARTETTE.—Miss Rainforth, Miss Julia Smith, Mr. Braham, and
　　Mr. John Parry.　　"Hear me when I swear."
SONG.—Mr. Braham.　　　　"There's a charm in Spring."
AIR.—Mr. John Parry.　　　"My Fair Home."
DUET.—Mr. Bennett and Mr. Braham.　"Listen, though I do
　　　　　　　　　　　　　　　　　not fear you."
SONG.—Miss Rainforth.　　"How Beautiful at Even Tide."
COUNTRY DANCE AND CHORUS.　"Join the Dance."
QUINTETTE.　　　　　　　　"No light bound."

FINALE.

The whole of the musical arrangements under the direction of
　　Mr G. Stansbury.
On this occasion, MR. HULLAH *will preside in the Orchestra.*

After which (50th time), an entirely new Burletta written by
"BOZ," called

THE STRANGE GENTLEMAN!

Mr. Owen Overton (*Mayor of a small
　town on the road to Gretna and useful
　at the St. James's Arms*) . . . Mr. Hollingsworth.
John Johnson (*detained at the St. James's
　Arms*) . . . . . . Mr. Sidney.
The Strange Gentleman (*just arrived at
　the St. James's Arms*) . . . Mr. Harley.
Charles Tomkins (*incognito at the St.
　James's Arms*) . . . . Mr. Forester.
Tom Sparks (*a one-eyed "Boots" at the
　St. James's Arms*) . . . . Mr. Gardner.
John, ⎫　　　　　　　　　　　⎧ Mr. Williamson.
Tom, ⎬ *waiters at the St. James's* ⎨ Mr. May.
Will, ⎭　　　　*Arms*　　　　　⎩ Mr. Coulson.
Julia Dobbs (*looking for a husband at the
　St. James's Arms*) . . . . Madame Sala.
Fanny Wilson (*with an appointment at
　the St. James's Arms*) . . . Miss Smith.
Mary Wilson (*her sister, awkwardly
　situated at the St. James's Arms*) . Miss Julia Smith.
Mrs. Noakes (*the landlady at the St.
　James's Arms*) . . . . Mrs. Penson.
Chambermaid (*at the St. James's Arms*) Miss Stuart.

The performance concluded with the performance of a burletta entitled "Delicate Attentions," and the playbills of the following day (December 7th, 1836), were headed with the following announcement:—

THE VILLAGE COQUETTES.

This Burletta experienced one of the most triumphant receptions ever known. The Piece was, in its progress, repeatedly loudly cheered, and the greater part of the Music was unanimously encored by a brilliant and crowded audience. It is needless to say more than it will be

REPEATED EVERY EVENING UNTIL FURTHER NOTICE!

The cast of "The Village Coquettes" remained unaltered, but on this occasion "The Strange Gentleman" was withdrawn from the bill, and its place taken by the "Humorous Burletta of Tom Thumb." The performance concluded as before, with "Delicate Attentions."

The following is an extract from the bill of the same theatre, dated March 14th, 1837, when "Is She His Wife" formed an item in the programme. The curtain rose on the representation of Adolph Adam's three-act "Operatic Burletta," called in its English dress "The Postillion."

After which an original comic Burletta in One Act, written by BOZ, called

IS SHE HIS WIFE? OR, SOMETHING SINGULAR!

Alfred Lovetown, Esq.	Mr. Forester.
Mr. Peter Limbury	Mr. Gardner.
Felix Tapkins, Esq. (*formerly of the India House, Leadenhall Street, and now of Rustic Lodge, near Reading*)	Mr. Harley.
Mrs. Lovetown	Miss Allison.
Mrs. Peter Limbury	Madame Sala.

Representations were also given of a two-act Operatic Burletta by Mrs. S. C. Hall, entitled "The French Refugee," and the still popular farce, "The Lottery Ticket."

Such programmes as these, contrast curiously with those at the St. James's Theatre of the present day, where, under the admirable management of Messrs. Hare and Kendal, and thanks mainly to the splendid acting of Mrs. Kendal, comedy representations are given second to none that have ever been seen either in this or any other country. As a sign of the changed habits of Londoners, it is noteworthy that in the days of the "Boz" pieces, the theatre doors were opened as early as half-past six, and the curtain rose punctually at seven o'clock. The prices then ranged from five shillings to eighteen-pence, with reduced second prices at "about nine o'clock." Certainly, as far as cost was concerned, the playgoer of 1836-7 could claim an advantage over us; but probably that advantage there ended.

Slight as they were, the pieces seem to have been very well received, as extracts from the dramatic criticisms of the day will show.

Here, for example, is an account, taken from the *Carlton Chronicle* of October 1st, 1836, of the first performance, at the St. James's Theatre, of "The Strange Gentleman":

"The entertainments commenced with a burletta from the pen of a gentleman who has very much amused the town by the broad humour and downright fun of sketches published by him under the *sobriquet* 'Boz.' 'The Strange Gentleman' is, we believe, founded upon one of his own stories, and it abounds in those strokes of quaintness, and happy perception and rich description of the ludicrous, for which his writings are remarkable. . . . A great number of mistakes occur; there is a great perplexity, and a number of accidents, which chiefly tend to the inconvenience and annoyance of the strange gentleman, who was personated by Mr. Harley, and who was accordingly, as to the *physique* and the performance, precisely what Mr. Harley is, in whatsoever character he may appear. . . . The piece was very well received throughout."

Speaking of the production of "The Village Coquettes," the same authority, on December 10, 1836, says:

"Mr. C. Dickens, who has made the town laugh so heartily by his 'right merrie' papers touching the Pickwick Club, has in the multiplicity of his literary occupations, found leisure to write the dramatic and lyric portion of an opera for this (the St. James's) Theatre. It is styled 'The Village Coquettes,' and when we add that the scene is laid one hundred years ago, it will be seen that the title is pregnant of the story. . . . For a simple village tale of this kind, written either as an accessory to the music, or as a vehicle for the melodies, a sparkling dialogue would be inappropriate; and still worse, it would have been thrown away in the mouths of actors, and the ears (comprehensive as they might be) of an audience come to hear music. Smoothness and sweetness of flowing sounds, was the great object to be attained in the lyric portion of a ballad opera relating to a passage of rustic life in England, 'all of the olden time.' . . . The music of the opera is very pretty, and Mr. Hullah, the composer, has given in it great promise of ability. The *mise en scène* was admirable—nothing could be better than the scenery and decorations. The dresses, too, were quaint and pleasing with the exception of the Squire's. Braham dressed him in a red velvet shooting-jacket, laced gorgeously. . . . Braham sung with great taste, feeling, and power. Miss Rainforth acquitted herself very creditably."

It is odd to read in these days of the brilliant librettos to which Mr. W. S. Gilbert has accustomed us, that a critic was once found who could declare that as "a vehicle for melodies, a sparkling dialogue would be inappropriate."

Assuredly the present day playgoer is more exacting, and a dull " book " has, before now, sealed the fate of an otherwise excellent operatic production.

" Mr. Nightingale's Diary," says Mr. Godfrey Turner, in an article entitled "' Boz' and the Play," which appeared in the *Theatre Magazine*, " written by Charles Dickens and Mark Lemon, served its purpose, and there an end. It is worth remarking, that the earliest attempts at authorship by Charles Dickens took a dramatic form. He, and his biographer, John Forster, both speak of certain nursery tragedies, achieved at the age of eight or ten." That these juvenile attempts (though, according to their author they were " represented with great applause to overflowing nurseries,") are inaccessible, goes without saying.

The writer is indebted to an interesting monograph from the pen of Mr. R. H. Shepherd for the following accumulated information respecting the production at the Adelphi Theatre, in December, 1867, of the dramatic version of " No Thoroughfare."

" It was on the eve of his second visit to America that Charles Dickens assisted in dramatising his story of ' No Thoroughfare,' written conjointly and in nearly equal portions with Mr. Wilkie Collins, to form the Christmas number of *All the Year Round* for 1867. In the midst of all the work of preparation for departure, the Editors of his Letters inform us, Charles Dickens gave minute attention to as much of the play as could be completed before he left England. It was 'the only story,' says Mr. Forster, 'he ever helped himself to dramatise.' The incidents are considerably changed in the drama, notably the scene in the Monastery in Act the Fifth, following Obenreizer's treachery on his fellow traveller, which concludes the Fourth Act. The clock-lock is placed in the monastery of St. Bernard, instead of in the house of a notary, as in the tale. The whole episode of Joey Ladle's courtship of Sally Goldstraw, and his admiration of her 'beautiful language,' is absent from the story and peculiar to the play, and contains some highly felicitous and characteristic Dickensian touches. Joey's muddled way of moralising, his intense affection for Sally Goldstraw, and his ludicrous attempts to commit her sayings to memory, relieve the otherwise somewhat sombre tone of the drama throughout, and make the honest cellarman a personage of much greater importance than he appears in the published story. The play indeed in some scenes departs from the story so widely as to be entitled to rank as an entirely original production. 'No Thoroughfare' was first produced at the Adelphi Theatre during Dickens's absence in the United States. It was first performed on

Boxing Night of 1867, Mr. Fechter taking the part of Obenreizer, and Mr. Webster that of Joey Ladle. Some allusions to the piece and to its favourable reception, when the news reached its absentee author, are scattered through Dickens's correspondence from America in the early part of 1868. From New York, early in January of that year, he thus writes to his collaborator, Mr. Wilkie Collins:—

"'New York, Sunday, Jan. 12, 1868.
"'First of the play. I am truly delighted to learn that it made so great a success, and I hope I may yet see it on the Adelphi boards. You have had a world of trouble and work with it, but I hope will be repaid in some degree by the pleasure of a triumph. Even for the alteration at the end of the Fourth Act I was fully prepared, for I COULD NOT see the original effect in the reading of the play, and COULD NOT make it go. I agree with Webster in thinking it best that Obenreizer should die on the stage; but no doubt that point is disposed of. In reading the play before the representation, I felt that it was too long, and that there was a good deal of unnecessary explanation. Those points are, no doubt, disposed of too by this time."

"To his eldest son a few days later, Dickens writes:

"'New York, Jan. 15, 1868.

"'I had previously heard of the play, and had the *Times*. It was a great relief and delight to me, for I had no confidence in its success, being reduced to the confines of despair by its length. If I could have rehearsed it, I should have taken the best part of an hour out of it. Fechter must be very fine, and I should greatly like to see him play the part.'

"To Fechter himself, who performed the character of Obenreizer, Dickens wrote (from Washington, February 24, 1868):

"'Wilkie," (*i.e.* Mr. Wilkie Collins) " has uniformly written of you enthusiastically. In a letter I had from him, dated the 10th of January, he described your conception and execution of the part in the most glowing terms. " Here Fechter is magnificent." " Here his superb playing brings the house down." " I should call even his exit in the last Act one of the subtlest and finest things he does in the piece." " You can hardly imagine what he gets out of the part, or what he makes of his passionate love for Marguerite." These expressions, and many others like them, crowded his letter. " I never did so want to see a character played on the stage as I want to see you play Obenreizer."

The popularity of "No Thoroughfare" at the Adelphi was beyond all question, as will be judged from the following conclusion to a notice which appeared in the now extinct satirical journal "The Mask," in which, previously, all the weak points in the play had been mercilessly pointed out, and most of the characters and their representatives roundly "chaffed":

"We heartily congratulate the management upon the great success of the new play. The old board on which is inscribed 'House full in every part,' after a long retirement among the lumber of the property-room, has again made its appearance; and, looking now quite fresh and beaming, hangs proudly under the portico every night. Charles Dickens and Wilkie Collins have made their dramatic hit at last! The first attempted it many years ago and failed. The second has attempted many times, and, as far as financial success is concerned, has failed also. In 'No Thoroughfare' they are both at liberty to enjoy their triumph to the utmost. It is a hit in every sense of the word, more particularly in the sense which is the pleasantest of all in managerial consideration. Its 'money' draw has never been equalled in the annals of the theatre."

This chapter would perhaps be incomplete without mention being made of a little play, which Dickens wrote in 1839 for Covent Garden, which the actors could not agree about, and which he turned afterwards into a story called "The Lamplighter." Writing in 1845, and speaking of his early desire to become an actor, and his interview with Mr. Bartley (mention of which is made in the next chapter), he said:

"I had an odd fancy, when I was reading the unfortunate little farce at Covent Garden, that Bartley looked as if some struggling recollection and connection were stirring up within him—but it may only have been his doubts of that humorous composition."

The manuscript of "The Lamplighter," in its dramatic form, but not in the handwriting of Dickens, is to be seen in the Forster collection at the South Kensington Museum. It is a curiously dull little piece, clumsily arranged in one act and three scenes, and the limited number of copies that were some years ago printed are interesting only to collectors. The best character in it is that of the Lamplighter, Tom Grig, who declares that when he grows rich he will have "a country house and a park,"—and "I'll plant a bit of it with a double row of gas lamps a mile long, and go out with a French-polished mahogany ladder, and two servants in livery behind me, to light 'em up with my own hands every night."

To the lover of the stage, and taking possibilities into consideration, this bald record of "Dickens as a Dramatist," seems sadly incomplete, but concerning his work in this direction there is practically nothing more to tell. The consolation is that, after all, he did do something in other ways!

CHAPTER IV.

DICKENS AS AN ACTOR.

In an article in *Longman's Magazine*, for May, 1883, Mr. Dutton Cook sums up the story told at length by Mr. Forster, of Dickens's early intention to become an actor.

"Early in life he had seriously contemplated the stage as a profession, and had even solicited an engagement at Covent Garden Theatre. He wrote to the stage manager, Mr. Bartley. 'I told him how young I was, and exactly what I thought I could do; that I believed I had a strong perception of character and oddity, and a natural power of reproducing in my own person what I observed in others.' Mr. Bartley made an appointment with his correspondent, then engaged at Doctors' Commons as a shorthand writer for the Proctors, in order to test his abilities; but when the time came Dickens was too ill with cold and inflammation of the face to appear. He had taken great pains, however, as he has related, to prepare himself for success as an actor. 'I went to some theatre every night, with a very few exceptions for at least three years, really studying the bills first, and going where there was the best acting, and always to see Mathews whenever he played. I practised immensely (even such things as walking in and out, and sitting down in a chair), often four, five, six hours a day, shut up in my own room or walking about in the fields. . . . I must have done a good deal, for, just as Macready found me out, they used to challenge me at Braham's; and Yates, who was knowing enough in these things, wasn't to be parried at all.' . . . . Dickens's literary successes soon induced him to abandon his intention of going upon the stage; as he said—he now 'did not want money, and he had never thought of the stage, but as a means of getting it.' Yet he could not but bear in mind, long afterwards, how near he had once been to 'another sort of life.' Nor could he ever relinquish his old fondness for the actor's art; for he scarcely did himself justice when he spoke of the stage as being to him but a means of getting money. He obtained great applause as an amateur actor, and he became famous as a public reader of his own books; his readings, in truth, closely resembling actings, or suggesting rather the readings of an actor than of an author. He was particular always on these occasions as to the arrangement of his gas-lights, that his expression and play of face might be properly seen and appraised. With this view a special 'gas-man,' ever accompanied him upon his tours in the provinces. He resorted to much 'stage business,' and employed sundry 'stage properties,' when he judged that he could in such wise the better enforce or illustrate the intention of his books. The copies of his stories from which he read in public were marked with as many 'stage directions,' as are contained in the acting editions of a play. When but a lad of sixteen, with a fellow-clerk in a lawyer's office, he is understood to have assumed certain characters at a minor theatre—probably one of those establishments supported entirely by amateur actors, such as then existed in Wilson Street, Gray's Inn Lane, and in Catherine Street, Strand." Such a theatre, in short, as the one described in the "Boz" sketches.

The first mention made by Mr. Forster of Dickens's subsequently famous connection with amateur theatricals, was in 1842, when, on the occasion of his first visit to America, he took part in some performances at Montreal. The pieces selected were "A Roland for an Oliver," "Past Two o'Clock in the Morning," and "Deaf as a Post"; and the characters undertaken by Dickens were respectively Alfred Highflyer, Mr. Snobbington, and Gallop. In addition to this, he was responsible for the duties of stage management and fulfilled them with characteristic thoroughness. "Didn't I come the Macready over them?" he wrote. "I had regular plots of the scenery made out, and lists of the properties wanted, and had them nailed up by the prompter's chair. Every letter that was to be delivered was written; every piece of money that had to be given, provided. I prompted myself, when I was not on; and when I was, I made the regular prompter of the theatre my deputy; and I never saw anything so perfectly touch-and-go as the first two pieces."

That the details of theatrical management had a peculiar fascination for him is instanced in the following anecdote, told by Mr. Charles Kent in his "Charles Dickens as a Reader." "Going round by way of Lambeth one afternoon," says Mr. Kent, "in the early summer of 1870, we had skirted the Thames along the Surrey bank, had crossed the river higher up, and, on our way back, were returning at our leisure through Westminster, when, just as we were approaching the shadow of the old Abbey at Poet's Corner, under the roof-beams of which he was so soon to be laid in his grave, with a rain of tears and flowers, he abruptly asked, 'What do you think would be the realisation of one of my most cherished day-dreams?' adding instantly, with-

7*

out waiting for my answer, 'To settle down for the remainder of my life within easy distance of a great theatre, in the direction of which I should hold supreme authority. It should be a house, of course, having a skilled and noble company, and one in every way magnificently appointed. The pieces acted should be dealt with according to my pleasure, and touched up here and there in obedience to my own judgment; the players as well as the plays being absolutely under my command. There,' said he, laughingly, and in a glow at the mere fancy, '*that's my day-dream!*'"

The success of the Canadian theatricals had evidently fired him with a desire to appear again behind the footlights, and to hold the managerial reins, and accordingly we find him, in 1847, entering heart and soul into the theatrical benefit organised on behalf of Leigh Hunt, and in which so many distinguished men took part. The general management and supreme control were given to Dickens, and the performances took place on the 26th July at Manchester, and the 28th July at Liverpool, Ben Jonson's comedy, "Every Man in His Humour" being followed on the first night by "A Good Night's Rest" and "Turning the Tables," and on the second by "Comfortable Lodgings, or, Paris in 1750."

In 1848, on behalf of the endowment of a

curatorship of Shakespeare's house at Stratford, the performance of the comedy was repeated in London. The following is a copy of the play-bill :—

THEATRE ROYAL, HAYMARKET.

Amateur Performance

in aid of

THE FUND FOR THE ENDOWMENT OF A PERPETUAL CURATORSHIP OF SHAKESPEARE'S HOUSE,

To be always held by some one distinguished in Literature, and more especially in Dramatic Literature ; the Profits of which it is the intention of the Shakespeare House Committee to keep entirely separate from the Fund now raising for the purchase of the House.

On Wednesday Evening, May 17th, 1848, will be presented
BEN JONSON'S Comedy of

EVERY MAN IN HIS HUMOUR.

Knowell (*an old gentleman*) . . . Mr. Dudley Costello.
Edward Knowell (*his son*) . . Mr. Frederick Dickens.
Brainworm (*the father's man*) . . Mr. Mark Lemon.
George Downwright (*a plain squire*) Mr. Frank Stone.
Wellbred (*his half-brother*) . . Mr. G. H. Lewes.
Kitely (*a merchant*) . . . . Mr. John Forster.
Captain Bobadil (*a Paul's man*) . . Mr. Charles Dickens.
Master Stephen (*a country gull*) . Mr. Augustus Egg.
Master Mathew (*the town gull*) . . Mr. John Leech.
Thomas Cash (*Kitely's cashier*) . Mr. Augustus Dickens.
Oliver Cobb (*a water bearer*) . . Mr. George Cruikshank.
Justice Clement (*an old merry magistrate*) . . . . . . Mr. Willmott.
Roger Formal (*his Clerk*) . . . Mr. Cole.
Dame Kitely (*Kitely's wife*) . . Miss Fortescue.
Mistress Bridget (*her sister*) . . Miss Kenworthy.
Tib (*Cobb's wife*) . . . . Mrs. Cowden Clarke.
The Costumes by Messrs. Nathan, of Titchbourne Street.

To conclude with Mr. Kenney's farce of

LOVE, LAW AND PHYSIC.

Doctor Camphor	Mr. George Cruikshank.
Captain Danvers	Mr. Frederick Dickens.
Flexible	Mr. Charles Dickens.
Andrew	Mr. G. H. Lewes.
Lubin Log	Mr. Mark Lemon.
John Brown	Mr. Augustus Egg.
Coachman	Mr. Eaton.
Laura	Miss Anne Romer.
Mrs. Hillary	Mrs. Cowden Clarke.
Chambermaid	Miss Woulds.

The Band will perform,

Previous to the Comedy, *The Overture to Semiramide* . Rossini

Between the Acts:
- *Battaglie Galop* . . . . Kolloonitsch.
- *Czarina Mazurka* . . . T. German Reed.
- *Aria Somnambula* { cornet obligato } Bellini.
- *Wedding March* . . . . Mendelssohn.

Previous to Farce, *The Prince of Wales Quadrilles* . Jullien

---

⁎⁎ *The doors will be opened at half-past six, and the performance will commence at half-past seven precisely, by which time it is requested that the whole of the company may be seated.*

Directors of general arrangements—Mr. John Payne Collier, Mr. Charles Knight, Mr. Peter Cunningham and the London Shakeseare House Committee.

Stage Manager—Mr. Charles Dickens.

Evening dress in all parts of the House.

"Great difficulty," Mr. Forster says, "was found in the selection of a suitable play to alternate with our old Ben Jonson. "The Alchemist" had been such a favourite with some of us, that, before finally laying it aside, we went through two or three rehearsals, in which I recollect thinking Dickens's Sir Epicure Mammon as good as anything he had done; and now the same trouble, with the same result, arising from a vain desire to please everybody, was taken successively with Beaumont and Fletcher's 'Beggar's Bush' and Goldsmith's 'Good-natured Man,' with Jerrold's characteristic drama of 'The Rent Day' and Bulwer's masterly comedy of 'Money.' Choice was at last made of Shakespeare's 'Merry Wives,' in which Lemon played Falstaff. I took again the jealous husband, as in Jonson's play, and Dickens was Justice Shallow; to which was added a farce, 'Love, Law, and Physic,' in which Dickens took the part he had acted long ago, before his days of authorship; and besides the professional actresses engaged, we had for our Dame Quickly the lady to whom the world owes incomparably the best 'Concordance to Shakespeare' that has ever been published, Mrs. Cowden Clarke. The success was undoubtedly very great. At Manchester, Liverpool and Edinburgh there were single representations, but Birmingham and Glasgow had each two nights, and two were given at the Haymarket, on one of which the Queen and Prince were present. The gross receipts from the nine performances, before the necessary large deductions for London and local charges, were two thousand five hundred and fifty-one pounds and eight pence."

Dickens, in his capacity as stage-manager, had

prepared a set of rules for rehearsals, from which the following is a quotation: "Remembering the very imperfect condition of all our plays at present, the general expectation in reference to them, the kind of audience before which they will be presented, and the near approach of the nights of performance, I hope everybody concerned will abide by the following regulations, and will aid in strictly carrying them out." . . . .
"Silence, on the stage and in the theatre, to be faithfully observed, the lobbies, &c., being always available for conversation. No book to be referred to on the stage; but those who are imperfect to take their words from the prompter. Everyone to act, as nearly as possible, as on the night of performance; everyone to speak out, so as to be audible through the house. And every mistake of exit, entrance, or situation to be corrected *three times* successively." . .

" All who were concerned in the first getting up of ' Every Man in his Humour,' and who remember how carefully the stage was always kept then, and who have been engaged in the late rehearsals of the ' Merry Wives,' and have experienced the difficulty of getting on or off, of being heard, or of hearing anybody else, will, I am sure, acknowledge the indispensable necessity of these regulations."

Mrs. Cowden Clarke, in the pleasant " Recollections of Writers," of which she and her husband are joint authors, naturally has much to say of these famous amateur performances. Speaking of the rehearsals, she says: "Charles Dickens, ever present, superintending, directing, suggesting, with sleepless activity and vigilance: the essence of punctuality and methodical precision himself, he kept incessant watch that others should be unfailingly attentive and careful throughout. Unlike most professional rehearsals, where waiting about, dawdling, and losing time, seem to be the order of the day, the rehearsals under Charles Dickens's stage-managership were strictly devoted to work— serious, earnest work; the consequence was that when the evening of performance came, the pieces went off with a smoothness and polish that belong only to finished stage-business and practised performers. He was always there among the first arrivers at rehearsals, and remained in a conspicuous position during their progress till the very last moment of conclusion. He had a small table placed rather to one side of the stage, at which he generally sat, as the scenes went on in which he himself took no part. On this table rested a moderate sized box, its interior divided into convenient compartments for holding papers, letters, etc., and this interior was always the very pink of neatness and orderly arrangement. Occasionally he would leave his seat at the managerial table, and stand with his back to the footlights in the very centre of the front of the stage, and view the whole effect of the rehearsed performance as it proceeded, observing the attitudes and positions of those engaged in the dialogue, their mode of entrance, exit, etc., etc. He never seemed to overlook anything, but to note the very slightest point that conduced to the 'going well' of the whole performance. With all this supervision, however, it was pleasant to remark the utter absence of dictatorialness or arrogation of superiority that distinguished his mode of ruling his troop: he exerted his authority firmly and perpetually, but in such a manner as to make it universally felt to be for no purpose of self-assertion or self-importance; on the contrary, to be for the sole purpose of ensuring general success to their united efforts."

As an instance of his attention to detail Mrs. Cowden-Clarke speaks of the card bearing the words, "Pass to the Stage: Charles Dickens," "with the emphatic scribble beneath his name, which formed the magic order for entrance through the stage-door of the theatre." The compiler of these pages is fortunate enough to be able to reproduce a copy of this card in facsimile.

> 12th May 1848
>
> Mr. Chas. Dickens.
>
> Every Man in his Humour
>
> Love, law & Physic
>
> 1. Devonshire Terrace. York Gate. Regents Park.

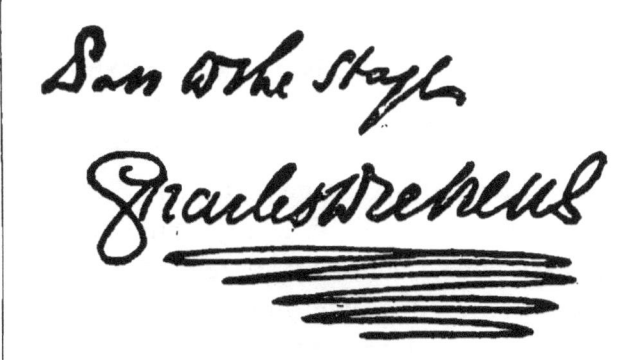

"The 'make-up' of Dickens as Justice Shallow," Mrs. Cowden-Clarke goes on to say, "was so complete, that his own identity was almost unrecognisable, when he came on to the stage, as the curtain rose, in company with Sir Hugh and Master Slender; but after a moment's breathless pause, the whole house burst forth into a roar of applausive reception, which testified to the boundless delight of the assembled audience on beholding the literary idol of the day, actually before them. His impersonation was perfect: the old, stiff limbs, the senile stoop of the shoulders, the head bent with age, the feeble step, with a certain attempted smartness of carriage characteristic of the conceited Justice of the Peace—were all assumed and maintained with wonderful accuracy; while the articulation, part lisp, part thickness of utterance, part a kind of impeded sibilation, like that of a voice that 'pipes and whistles in the sound' through loss of teeth—gave consummate effect to his mode of speech. The one in which Shallow says, ' 'Tis the heart, Master Page; 'tis here, 'tis here. I have seen the time with my long sword I would have made you four tall fellows skip like rats,' was delivered with a humour of expression in effete energy of action and would-be fire of spirit that marvellously imaged fourscore years in its attempt to denote vigour long since extinct."

Of Dickens's performance in 'Every Man in His Humour,' the same writer says: "The way in which Charles Dickens impersonated that arch braggart, Captain Bobadil, was a veritable piece of genius: from the moment when he is discovered lolling at full length on a bench in his lodgings, calling for a 'cup o' small beer' to cool down the remnants of excitement from last night's carouse with a set of roaring gallants, to his final boast of having 'not so much as once offered to resist' the 'coarse fellow' who set upon him in the open streets, he was capital. The mode in which he went to the back of the stage before he made his exit from the first scene of Act II., uttering the last word of the taunt he flings at Downright with a bawl of stentorian loudness, 'Scavenger!' and then darted off the stage at full speed; the insolent scorn of his exclamation, 'This a Toledo? pish!' bending the sword into a curve as he spoke; the swaggering assumption of ease with which he leaned on the shoulder of his interlocutor, puffing away his tobacco smoke and puffing it off as 'your right Trinidado!' the grand impudence of his lying when explaining how he would despatch scores of the enemy—'challenge twenty more, kill them; twenty more, kill them; twenty more, kill them too'; ending by 'twenty score, that's two hundred; two hundred a day, five days a thousand; forty thousand; forty times five, five times forty, two hundred days kills them all up by computation,' rattling the words off while making an invisible sum of addition in the air, and scoring it conclusively with an invisible line underneath—were all the very height of fun."

Speaking of his performance in " Used Up," our authority says " Charles Dickens's Sir Charles Coldstream was excellent."

"The Farce of ' Love, Law and Physic,'" Mrs. Cowden-Clarke continues, "was a large field for the very hey-day of frolic and mirth. . . . . In token of Charles Dickens's appropriateness of gesture, and dramatic discrimination, I may instance his different mode of entrance on the stage with me as Mrs. Quickly and as Mrs. Hillary. Where Justice Shallow comes hurriedly in with the former, Act III., Scene 4, saying to her 'Break their talk, Mistress Quickly;' he used to have hold of my arm, partly leaning on it, partly leading me on by it, just like an old man with an inferior; but, as the curtain rose to the ringing of bells, the clattering of horses, the blowing of mail coach horn, the voices of passengers calling to waiter and chambermaid, &c., at the opening of 'Love, Law and Physic,' Charles Dickens used to tuck me under his arm with the free-and-easy familiarity of a lawyer patronising an actress whom he chances to find his fellow traveller in a stage coach, and step smartly on to the stage, with 'Come, bustle, bustle; tea and coffee for the ladies.' It is something to remember, having been tucked under the arm by Charles Dickens, and had one's hand hugged against his side! One thinks better of one's hand ever after."

Abundant evidence is forthcoming of the success of Dickens's acting on this occasion. His Captain Bobadil was thus spoken of by one of the leading critics of the day: "Such a Bobadil as that of Mr. Dickens had not been seen within the memory of man. I well remember the change which, according to his interpretation, took place in the character of the braggart after he had received his cudgelling. Before the beating he was so gallant and jaunty; after it, his very soul appeared to be crushed within him. Even his bodily identity was altered. The general feeling among the audience was compassion for the crest-fallen captain, which the dramatist had scarcely intended to inspire. 'I almost wish he had not been beaten,' was the exclamation that circulated among the fairer portion of the brilliant audience."

The same writer adds: "Well as the comedy was performed, and great as was the interest caused by the first appearance of so many gentlemen eminent in literature on the stage of a theatre, the unsuitability of the work to modern audiences could not be concealed. Lord Melbourne, a man of decided theatrical proclivities, occupied a private box, and was heard to say in a too audible whisper, 'I knew this comedy was dull, but I did not think it was so d——d dull.'"

The next of these " splendid strollings," as the performances were by no means inappropriately dubbed, were given after an interval of about two years.

"At the close of November, 1850," says Mr. Forster, "in the great hall of Lord Lytton's old family mansion in Knebworth Park, there were three private performances by the original actors in 'Every Man in his Humour.' All the circumstances and surroundings were very brilliant; some of the gentlemen of the county played both in the comedy and farces; our generous host was profuse of all noble encouragement, and amid the general pleasure and excitement hopes rose high."

The following is a copy of the play-bill :—

KNEBWORTH.

On Monday, November 18th, 1850,
will be performed, Ben Jonson's comedy of

EVERY MAN IN HIS HUMOUR.

Costumiers.—Messrs. Nathan, of Titchbourne street.
Perruquier.—Mr. Wilson, of the Strand.

Knowell (*an old gentleman*)	Mr. Delmé Radcliffe.
Edward Knowell (*his son*)	Mr. Henry Hawkins.

Brainworm (*the father's man*)	Mr. Mark Lemon.
George Downright (*a plain Squire*)	Mr. Frank Stone.
Wellbred (*his half-brother*)	Mr. Henry Hale.
Kitely (*a merchant*)	Mr. John Forster.
Captain Bobadil (*a Paul's man*)	Mr. Charles Dickens.
Master Stephen (*a country gull*)	Mr. Douglas Jerrold.
Master Matthew (*the town gull*)	Mr. John Leech.
Thomas Cash (*Kitely's cashier*)	Mr. Frederick Dickens.
Oliver Cobb (*a water-bearer*)	Mr. Augustus Egg.
Justice Clement (*an old merry magistrate*)	The Hon. Eliot Yorke.
Roger Formal (*his clerk*)	Mr. Phantom.
Dame Kitely (*Kitely's wife*)	Miss Anne Romer.
Mistress Bridget (*his sister*)	Miss Hogarth.
Tib (*Cob's wife*)	Mrs. Mark Lemon.

(Who has kindly consented to act in lieu of MRS. CHARLES DICKENS, disabled by an accident).

The Epilogue by Mr. Delmé Radcliffe.

To conclude with Mrs. Inchbald's farce of

ANIMAL MAGNETISM.

The Doctor	Mr. Charles Dickens.
La Fleur	Mr. Mark Lemon.
The Marquis de Lancy	Mr. John Leech.
Jeffery	Mr. Augustus Egg.
Constance	Miss Hogarth.
Lisette	Miss Anne Romer.
Stage Manager	Mr. Charles Dickens.

The theatre will be open at half past six. The performance will begin precisely at half-past seven.

GOD SAVE THE QUEEN!

The Epilogue, by Mr. F. P. Delmé Radcliffe, allusion to which is here made, takes the form of a rhymed dialogue between old Knowell and Wellbred. All the characters in the play are referred to, and the mention of Dickens is made as follows:

"Amongst the party there *are* pretty pickin's!

But say, can newspaper describe Charles
 Dickens?
Author and actor; manager; the soul
Of all who read or hear him! on the whole
A very *Household Word*."

Reference is also made to the accident which prevented the appearance of Mrs. Dickens:

Wellbred. Now, how about the ladies?
Knowell. For my part
I have got *their* perfections all by heart.
Wellbred. Hush! What would Dickens say
 to such sweet word?
Knowell. Why, that the lady emulates her
 lord.
A word on her sad accident; but quite
Impromptu, not intended for to-night.
Oh, may she soon recover from her sprain,
To tread with us, her friends, these boards
 again!
Wellbred. That fall sank all our spirits;- but
 in need,
'Tis said, a friend is found a friend indeed.
Successful friendship has our cares allayed—
Knowell. Ay, and the case relieved by *Lemon-
 aid.*

Out of these Knebworth performances sprang the idea of the "Guild of Literature and Art," and the determination to give, on behalf of its endowment, another series of amateur entertainments. A five-act comedy was to be written by Sir Edward Lytton, and when a certain sum of money had been obtained by public representations of it, the details of the scheme were to be drawn up, and appeal made to those whom it addressed more especially. "In a very few months," writes Mr. Forster, "everything was ready, except a farce which Dickens was to have written to follow the comedy, and which unexpected cares of management and preparation were held to absolve him from. There were other reasons. 'I have written the first scene,' he wrote, 'and it has droll points in it, more farcical points than you commonly find in farces—really better. Yet I am constantly striving, for my reputation's sake, to get into a meaning that is impossible in a farce; constantly thinking of it, therefore, against the grain, and constantly impressed with a conviction that I could never act in it myself with that wild abandonment which can alone carry a farce off. Wherefore I have confessed to Bulwer Lytton, and asked for absolution.' There was substituted a new farce of Lemon's, to which, however, Dickens soon contributed so many jokes and so much Gampish and other fun of his own, that it came to be in effect, a joint piece of authorship." This was the little play already alluded to in these pages, and subsequently made famous as "Mr. Nightingale's Diary."

The first performance of the new programme took place at Devonshire House, on the 27th of May, 1851, before the Queen and Prince and as large an audience as places could be found for. The success was considerable, and, after a series of representations at the Hanover Square Rooms, strolling began in the country. A copy of one of the play-bills is here given :—

HANOVER SQUARE ROOMS.

On Wednesday Evening, June 18th, 1851,

The Amateur Company of the Guild of Literature and Art,

To encourage Life Assurance and other Provident habits among Authors and Artists; to render such assistance to both as shall never compromise their independence; and to found a new Institution where honourable rest from arduous labour shall still be associated with the discharge of congenial duties;

Will have the Honour of Performing, for the THIRD TIME, a New Comedy, in Five Acts, by SIR EDWARD BULWER LYTTON, Bart., called

NOT SO BAD AS WE SEEM;

or,

MANY SIDES TO A CHARACTER :

The Duke of Middlesex } *Peers attached to the son of James II., commonly called the First Pretender* } Mr. Frank Stone.
The Earl of Loftus } Mr. Dudley Costello.
Lord Wilmot (*a young Man at the head of the Mode more than a century ago, son to Lord Loftus*) . . . . Mr. Charles Dickens.
Mr. Shadowly Softhead (*a young gentleman from the City, Friend and Double to Lord Wilmot*) . . . . Mr. Douglas Jerrold.

DICKENS AS AN ACTOR. 117

Mr. Hardman (*a Rising Member of Parliament and Adherent to Sir Robert Walpole*) . . . . . Mr. John Forster.
Sir Geoffrey Thornside (*a gentleman of good family and estate*) . . . Mr. Mark Lemon.
Mr. Goodenough Easy (*in business, highly respectable, and a friend of Sir Geoffrey*) . . . . . Mr. F. W. Topham.
Lord Le Trimmer . . . Mr. Peter Cunningham.
Sir Thomas Timid . . . . . Mr. Westland Marston.
Colonel Flint . . . . . Mr. R. H. Horne.
Mr. Jacob Tonson (*a bookseller*) . . Mr. Charles Knight.
Smart (*valet to Lord Wilmot*) . . Mr. Wilkie Collins.
Hodge (*servant to Sir Geoffrey Thornside*) . . . . . Mr. John Tenniel.
Paddy O'Sullivan (*Mr. Fallen's landlord*) . . . . . Mr. Robert Bell.
Mr. David Fallen (*Grub Street author and pamphleteer*) . . . Mr. Augustus Egg.

Lord Strongbow, Sir John Bruin, Coffee-House Loungers, Drawers, Watchmen and Newsmen.

Lucy (*daughter to Sir Geoffrey Thornside*) . . . . . Mrs. Henry Compton.
Barbara (*daughter to Mr. Easy*) . . Miss Young.
The Silent Lady of Deadman's Lane . Mrs. Coe.

SCENERY.

Lord Wilmot's Lodgings . . Painted by Mr. Pitt.
"The Murillo" . . . ,, Mr. Absalom.
Sir Geoffrey Thornside's Library . ,, Mr. Pitt.
Will's Coffee-house . . . ,, Mr. Pitt.
The Streets and Deadman's Lane . ,, Mr. Thomas Grieve.
The Distrest Poet's Garret (*after Hogarth*) . . . . ,, Mr. Pitt.
The Mall in the Park . . ,, Mr. Telbin.
An Open Space near the River . ,, Mr. Stanfield, R.A.
Tapestry Chamber in Deadman's Lane . . . . . ,, Mr. Louis Haghe.
The Act Drop . . . . ,, Mr. Roberts, R.A.

Previous to the Play, the Band will perform, under the direction of Mr. Lund, an Overture, composed expressly for this occasion by Mr. C. Coote, Pianist to His Grace the Duke of Devonshire.

The performance to conclude with (for the second time) an Original Farce, in One Act, by Mr. Charles Dickens and Mr. Mark Lemon, entitled

MR. NIGHTINGALE'S DIARY:

Mr. Nightingale	. Mr. Dudley Costello.
Mr. Gabblewig (*of the Middle Temple*)	. Mr. Charles Dickens.
Tip (*his Tiger*)	. Mr. Augustus Egg.
Slap (*professionally Mr. Flormiville*) .	. Mr. Mark Lemon.
Lithers (*landlord of the " Water-Lily "*)	. Mr. Wilkie Collins.
Rosina	. Miss Young.
Susan	. Mrs. Coe.

The Proscenium by Mr. Crace. The Theatre constructed by Mr. Sloman, machinist of the Royal Lyceum Theatre. The Properties and Appointments by Mr. G. Foster. The Costumes (with the exception of the Ladies' dresses, and the dresses of the Farce, which are by Messrs. Nathan, of Titchborne Street) made by Mr. Barnett, of the Theatre Royal, Haymarket. Under the superintendence of Mr. Augustus Egg, A.R.A. Perruquier, Mr. Wilson, of the Strand. Prompter, Mr. Coe.

———o———
The whole Produced under the Direction of Mr. CHARLES DICKENS.
———o———
The Band will be under the Direction of Mr. LUND.

Tickets (all the seats being reserved), 10s. each, to be had of Mr. Sams, 1, St. James's Street).

Doors open at a Quarter before SEVEN; commence at exactly a Quarter before EIGHT. The whole of the audience are particularly recommended to be seated before a Quarter to Eight.

Notwithstanding the immense attraction of its cast, and the undoubted success of the enterprise in which it was concerned, it is very much to be doubted whether " Not so Bad as We Seem " was the happiest selection that the amateurs could have made. That, after a few performances, " alterations " (ill omen to the dramatic author !) were found necessary is evident.

In the edition of the comedy published in 1851, by Messrs. Chapman and Hall, for the Guild of Literature and Art, the following "slip" notice was inserted:

"The length of this Play necessitates (as in 'Richelieu') many omissions in stage representations. The most important, as regards business and plot, is that of the concluding scene in the fourth act. By the omission of this scene, the agency of Softhead in obtaining from the Duke of Middlesex the Requisition to the Pretender is suppressed. And Hardman is introduced (Scene i. Act v.) as having obtained that important packet from Fallen's messenger.

"The place named in the printed Play for the Duke's appointment with the Messenger, is changed in the acting, from the wall by Lord Berkeley's garden to the river-side, behind Ranelagh; a change that the spectator will comprehend and appreciate when he sees the beautiful river scene, which forms Mr. Stanfield's generous contribution to the purposes for which this Play is composed and performed."

It seems more than likely that the master-hand of Dickens had something to do with these eminently practical, and diplomatically brought about "cuts."

In Mr. R. H. Horne's "Recollections of Contemporaries," associated with the *Gentleman's Magazine*, and which are comprised with the delightful "Letters of Elizabeth Barrett Browning," will be found the following account of the Devonshire House performance:

"The Duke gave us the use of his large picture gallery, to be fitted up with seats for the audience; and his library adjoining for the erection of the theatre. The latter room being longer than required for the stage and the scenery, the back portion of it was screened off for a "green room." Sir Joseph Paxton was most careful in the erection of the theatre and seats. There was a special box for the Queen. None of the valuable paintings in the picture gallery (arranged for the auditorium) were removed; but all were faced with planks, and covered with crimson velvet draperies; not a nail was allowed to be hammered into the floor or walls, the lateral supports being by the pressure from end to end, of padded beams; and the uprights, or stanchions, were fitted with iron feet, firmly fixed to the floor by copper screws. The lamps and their oil were well considered, so that the smoke should not be offensive or injurious—even the oil being slightly scented—and there was a profusion of wax candles. Sir Joseph Paxton also arranged the ventilation in the most skilful manner; and, with some assistance from a theatrical machinist, he put up all the scenes, curtains, and flies. Dickens was unanimously chosen general manager, and Mark Lemon stage manager. We had a professional gentleman for prompter, as none of the amateurs could be entrusted with so technical, ticklish, and momentous a duty.

"Never in the world of theatres was a better manager than Charles Dickens. Without, of course, questioning the superiority of Goethe (in the Weimar theatre) as a manager in all matters of high-class dramatic literature, one cannot think he could have been so excellent in all general requirements, stage effects, and practical details. Equally assiduous and unwearying as Dickens, surely very few men ever were, or could possibly be. He appeared almost ubiquitous and sleepless."

Speaking of Dickens's acting in " Not so Bad as we Seem," Mr. Horne says:

" The character and costume of 'Lord Wilmot, a young man *at the head of the Mode*, more than a century ago,' did not suit him. His bearing on the stage, and the tone of his voice, were too rigid, hard, and quarter-deck-like, for such 'rank and fashion,' and his make-up, with the three-cornered, gold-laced, cocked hat, black curled wig, huge sleeve cuffs, long flapped waistcoat, knee-breeches and shoe-buckles, were not carried off with the proper air; so that he would have made a good portrait of a captain of a Dutch privateer, after having taken a capital prize. When he shouted in praise of the wine of Burgundy it far rather suggested fine kegs of Schiedam."

In "Mr. Nightingale's Diary," however, a great success was obtained. This little piece had hardly any plot, and appears to have been somewhat of the nature of what is, now-a-days, known as a "variety entertainment." In it Dickens appeared in five different characters, namely: Sam Weller; Mr. Gabblewig, an over-voluble barrister; a hypochondriac; Mrs. Gamp, ("not the real Mrs. Gamp, but only a near relation"); and an old sexton, ninety years of age. He also took part in a broadsword combat, fought *à la* Crummles.

In a critical account of these performances which appeared in *Bentley's Miscellany* for June, 1851, great praise is bestowed upon Dickens's impersonation of this Mrs. Gamp-like character.

Fascinating as the public actor's life, without doubt, was to a man of Dickens's temperament, it was some time, unless we except home performances devised for the entertainment of his children, before he again appeared upon the boards. But how excellent these back-drawing-room productions must have been! "Carrying memory back to his home in the first half of 1854," says Mr. Forster, "there are few things that arise more pleasantly in connection with it than the children's theatricals. These began with the first Twelfth Night at Tavistock House, and were renewed until the principal actors ceased to be children. The best of the performances were 'Tom Thumb' and 'Fortunio,' in '54 and '55; Dickens now joining first in the revel, and Mr. Mark Lemon bringing into it his own clever children and a very mountain of child-pleasing fun in himself. In Fielding's burlesque he was the giantess Glumdalca, and Dickens was the ghost of Gaffer Thumb; the names by which they respectively appeared, being the Infant Phenomenon and the Modern Garrick. . . . In 'Fortunio' (Twelfth Night, 1855) Dickens played the testy Old Baron, and took advantage of the excitement against the Czar, then raging, to denounce him (in a song) as no other than own cousin to the very Bear that Fortunio had gone forth to subdue. He depicted him, in his desolation of autocracy, as the Robinson Crusoe of absolute state, who had at his court many a show-day, and many a high-day, but hadn't in all his dominions a Friday. The bill, which attributed these interpolations to 'the Dramatic Poet of the Establishment,' deserves also mention for the fun of the six large-lettered announcements which stood at the head of it, and could not have been bettered by Mr. Crummles himself. 'Re-engagement of that irresistible comedian Mr. Ainger!' 'Re-appearance of Mr. H. who created so powerful an impression last year!' 'Return of Mr. Charles

Dickens, Jun., from his German engagements!'
'Engagement of Miss Kate, who declined the munificent offers of the Management last season!' Mr. Passé, Mr. Mudperiod, Mr. Measly Servile, and Mr. Wilkini Collini!' 'First appearance on any stage of Mr. Plornishmaroontigoonter (who has been kept out of bed at a vast expense).' The last performer mentioned was yet some distance from the third year of his age. Dickens was Mr. Passé."

In 1855, Tavistock House was the scene of private theatricals on a far more ambitious scale. Mr. Wilkie Collins's play, "The Lighthouse," being performed with a degree of excellence and completeness rarely surpassed in any theatre, and with a success that naturally led to its production elsewhere.

In his "Journal of a London Playgoer," Mr. Henry Morley thus speaks of one of the private performances of this dramatic work:—

"*July* 14*th*, 1855.—On Tuesday evening, at Campden House, Kensington, the residence of Colonel Waugh, semi-private theatricals were given, with a charitable purpose, and with striking success, under the management of Mr. Charles Dickens."

"At Campden House there is a miniature theatre, complete with pit and boxes, stage and footlights. For the benefit of the funds of the Bournemouth Sanatorium for Consumptive Patients, the amateurs performed in this little theatre before a crowded audience, composed principally of ladies, a new two-act play by Mr. Wilkie Collins, and a two-act farce. The play was called 'The Lighthouse,' and told a tale of Eddystone in the old times. An exquisite picture (for such it is, and not a mere ordinary scene) of Eddystone as it stood in those days, from the pencil of Mr. Stanfield, was the drop-scene, and the actors were exhibited throughout as shut up in a little room within the lighthouse, also of Mr. Stanfield's painting, which, from its nature, could with the best possible effect be set up in a private drawing-room, or on a minature stage. Similar exigencies appear also to have been consulted in the manner of developing the plot of the play; the crime, the wreck, and all the events upon which hangs the passion of the story, not being produced upon the scene, but breaking out from the narration of the actors. None of the leading incidents are shown actually, but their workings on the minds of the three lighthousemen who are the chief performers, and of the few other persons introduced into the story, contribute interest enough to sustain an earnest attention throughout. The little piece told upon the audience admirably."

"But it had rare advantages. It was, in its principal parts, acted by distinguished writers, with whose artistic skill upon the stage the public has been for some time familiar. The three lighthouse-men are at first shown cut off by a month's storm from the mainland. They are an old man and his son, together with the father of the young man's sweetheart. The old man's memory is haunted by what he believes to have been his passive consent to a most foul murder. Weakened by starvation, his brain becomes wholly possessed by dread of this crime. The spectre of the supposed murdered lady seems to stand at his bedside and bid him speak. He does speak, and, possessed with a wild horror at all he recollects, reveals to his son his shame. Upon the acting of this character depends the whole force of the story, as presented to the audience, and it is in the hands of a master. He is a rough man, whose face has been familiar for years with wind and spray, haggard and wild just now, and something light-headed, oppressed not more by conscience than by hunger. He tells his tale and his son turns from him, shrinks from his touch, struck down by horror of the crime, and the humiliation to himself involved in it. Relief comes to the party soon after this; they are fed, and the physical depression is removed. Eager then to regain his son's esteem, and cancel the disclosure of his secret, the old lighthouse-man changes in manner. By innumerable master-touches on the part of the actor, we are shown what his rugged ways have been of hiding up the knowledge that stirs actively within his conscience; but his effort to be bold produces only nervous bluster, and his frantic desire to recover his son's respect, though he may take him by the throat to extort it from him, is still mixed up with a horrible sense of blood-guiltiness, wonderfully expressed by little instinctive actions. I will not follow the story to its last impressive moment of rough, nervous, seaman's prayer, in which the old man stands erect, with his hands joined over his head, overpowered by the sudden removal of the load that has so long weighed upon his heart. But to the last that piece of the truest acting was watched with minute attention by the company assembled; and rarely has acting on a public stage better rewarded scrutiny."

The actor, of course, was Dickens, and it is worth noting that Carlyle compared his wild picturesqueness in this exacting part to the famous figure in Nicholas Poussin's bacchanalian dance in the National Gallery.

Mr. Clarkson Stanfield's "Lighthouse" actdrop subsequently decorated the walls at Gad's Hill, and although it took the great painter less than a couple of days to execute, fetched 1,000 guineas at the famous Dickens sale of 1870. A cloth painted for the " Frozen Deep" which was the next and last of these productions, also had a prominent place in the Gad's Hill picture gallery.

" The Lighthouse" was subsequently produced at the Olympic Theatre, under the management of Messrs. Robson and Emden, and with Mr. F. Robson in the leading part.

Mrs. Cowden Clarke was much struck by Dickens's performance in " The Lighthouse." Of it she says:

" Later on in the scene a low planked recess in the wall is opened, where Charles Dickens—as the first lighthouse keeper, an old man with half-dazed wits and a bewildered sense of some wrong committed in bygone years—is discovered asleep in his berth. A wonderful impersonation was this; very imaginative, very original, very wild, very striking; his grandly intelligent eyes were made to assume a wandering look,—a sad, scared lost gaze, as of one whose spirit was away from present objects, and wholly occupied with absent and long-past images."

About a year later on Mr. Wilkie Collins's drama, " The Frozen Deep," was performed with equally gratifying results, and in some introductory lines that preface this powerful story as told in narrative form its author writes:

" As long ago as the year 1856, I wrote a play called 'The Frozen Deep.'

"The work was first represented by amateur actors, at the house of the late Charles Dickens, on the 6th of January, 1857. Mr. Dickens himself played the principal part, and played it with a truth, vigour and pathos never to be forgotten by those who were fortunate enough to witness the performance. The other personages of the story were represented by the ladies of Mr. Dickens's family, by the late Mark Lemon, by the late Augustus Egg, R.A., and by the author."

" The next appearance of 'The Frozen Deep,' (played by the Amateur Company) took place at the Gallery of Illustration, Regent Street, before the Queen and the Royal Family, by the Queen's own command. After this special performance other representations of the work were given— first at the Gallery of Illustration, subsequently with professional actresses, in some of the principal towns in England—for the benefit of the family of a well-loved friend of ours, who died in 1857, the late Douglas Jerrold. At Manchester the play was twice performed—on the second evening in the presence of three thousand spectators. This was, I think, the finest of all the representations of 'The Frozen Deep.' The extraordinary intelligence and enthusiasm of the great audience stimulated us all to do our best. Dickens surpassed himself. The trite phrase is the true phrase to describe that magnificent piece of acting. He literally electrified the audience."

The following is a copy of a portion of the original playbill of this memorable performance.

In remembrance of the late Mr. Douglas Jerrold.

FREE TRADE HALL.

UNDER THE MANAGEMENT OF MR. CHARLES DICKENS.

On FRIDAY Evening August 21st, and on SATURDAY Evening August 22nd, 1857,

AT EIGHT O'CLOCK EXACTLY,

Will be presented an entirely New Romantic Drama in Three Acts, by

MR. WILKIE COLLINS.
CALLED
THE FROZEN DEEP.

The Overture composed expressly for this piece by Mr. Francesco Berger, who will conduct the Orchestra.

Captain Edsworth (*of the "Sea Mew"*)   Mr. Edward Pigott.
Captain Helding (*of the "Wanderer"*)   Mr. Alfred Dickens
Lieutenant Crayford . . . Mr. Mark Lemon.
Frank Aldersley . . . . Mr. Wilkie Collins.
Richard Wardour . . . . Mr. Charles Dickens.
Lieutenant Steventon . . . Mr. Young Charles. *
John Want (*Ship's Cook*) . . Mr. Augustus Egg.
Bateson } (*two of the " Sea-Mew's "* { Mr. Shirley Brooks.
Darker }   *People*) { Mr. Charles Collins.

Officers and Crews of the "Sea-Mew," and "Wanderer."

Mrs. Steventon . . . . . Mrs. George Vining.
Rose Ebsworth . . . . Miss Ellen Sabine.
Lucy Crayford . . . . Miss Ellen Ternan.
Clara Burnham . . . . Miss Maria Ternan.
Nurse Esther . . . . . Mrs. Ternan.
Maid . . . . . . Miss Mewte. †

The Scenery and Scenic Effects of the First Act, by MR. TELBIN.
The Scenery and Scenic Effects of the Second and Third Acts, by MR. STANFIELD, R.A.

* A facetious nickname invented by Dickens for his eldest son.
† Another nickname by Dickens for a young lady who had nothing to say.

Ten years after this "The Frozen Deep" was professionally performed at the Olympic Theatre, with Mr. Henry Neville in the part "created" by Dickens.

Considering that the greater part of its action takes place in the Arctic regions, the mounting of Mr. Wilkie Collins's play was no light undertaking for the amateur stage, but this is as nothing compared with the successful interpretation of the character of Richard Wardour by one who called himself an amateur actor. The dramatist has depicted Wardour as a man swayed by the most intense passions, placed by circumstances in positions of the most terrible trial. It is just one of those parts that bad or even indifferent acting of a melodramatic school would make ridiculous. But in the hands of Dickens it became a magnificent human study, and lifted the play, and all concerned in it, into a splendid artistic success.

To these performances of Mr. Wilkie Collins's drama, an incalculably great and ever-increasing audience is indebted.

In the preface to "A Tale of Two Cities," Dickens says: "When I was acting with my children and friends, in Mr. Wilkie Collins's drama of 'The Frozen Deep,' I first conceived the main idea of this story. A strong desire was upon me then, to embody it in my own person;

9*

and I traced out in my fancy, the state of mind of which it would necessitate the presentation to an observant spectator, with particular care and interest."

The character he desired to play was of course that of Sydney Carton.

"As the idea became familiar to me," he goes on to say, "it gradually shaped itself into its present form. Throughout its execution it had complete possession of me; I have so far verified what is done and suffered in these pages, as that I have certainly done and suffered it all myself."

He sent the proof-sheets of the story to his friend Regnier of the Théâtre Français, and wrote: "I should very much like to know what you think of its being dramatised for a French theatre."

Regnier replied that, as he judged, such a play would be prohibited by the authorities.

To Miss Mary Boyle, Dickens wrote: "I must say that I like my Carton, and I have a faint idea sometimes that if I had acted him, I could do something with his life and death."

A dramatic version of the novel was prepared by Mr. Tom Taylor, and produced at the Lyceum under Madame Celeste's management, with but scant success.

A critical and very interesting account of "Mr. Dicken'ss Amateur Theatricals" appeared in *Mac-*

millan's Magazine for January, 1871, and the writer thus expresses his opinion of Dickens's acting abilities:

"To say that his acting was amateurish is to depreciate it in the view of a professional actor, but it is not necessarily to disparage it. No one who heard the public readings from his own books which Mr. Dickens subsequently gave with so much success, needs to be told what rare natural qualifications for the task he possessed. Fine features, and a striking presence, with a voice of great flexibility, were added to a perfect mastery over the sense of his author, because that author was himself. . . .

"If there was a certain ease and *handiness* which the practice of the art as a profession might have brought to him, he at least escaped the tyranny of those conventionalisms which the best actors (at least of our own time) have not been able to resist. Mr. Dickens's acting — certainly his *serious* acting — might have failed in a large theatre, just as a picture painted by Creswick or Cooke would have been ineffective if used as a scene in that theatre. In both cases, broader effects and less carefulness in details would have been needed to produce the desired effect."

That Dickens, with his comparatively limited experience, was not an absolutely perfect actor goes without saying, but that, had the study of the stage been the work of his life, he would have developed into a very great one, ample evidence has been given.

To this invaluable testimony is given by Mrs. Henry Compton, whose name was associated with the most brilliant performances given in the days of "splendid strolling." Mrs. Compton, who, as Miss Emmeline Montague, was recognised as one of the most accomplished and delightful actresses of those days, and who consequently speaks with no ordinary authority, says that though she was, on these occasions, appearing with "amateurs," she always felt that in playing with Dickens she had by her side an *actor* whose tact, talent, and resource would be equal to any emergency that might arise. She also tells how her gifted husband used to declare that had Dickens adopted the stage as a profession, he would have made upon it fame and fortune. As a proof of the pleasant manner in which all the arrangements of these performances were carried out, and in order to show the true delicacy with which Dickens conducted all business matters connected with them, Mrs. Compton most kindly allows the following letter to appear in these pages:

"Broadstairs, Kent.
"Fourteenth September, 1848.
"MY DEAR MISS MONTAGUE,
"Allow me to forward you, by favour of our

friend, Mark Lemon, the enclosed cheque, which is the mere business part of a crowd of pleasant remembrances I shall always associate with you, that are not to be coined into any sort of money I know of.

"Believe in my sincere interest in all that concerns your prosperity and happiness, and in the real satisfaction I shall have if I can ever testify it by any means of usefulness to you.

"Always faithfully yours,
"CHARLES DICKENS."
"Miss Emmeline Montague."

There is no doubt, however, that Dickens's greatest histrionic triumphs were achieved at the reading-desk. Those who are fortunate enough to be able to recall the cunningly contrived and admirably lighted platform, which was the outcome of his keen eye for theatrical effect, and to remember the mobile face, the expressive eye, and the deftly-managed voice, which, in turn, could conjure up love or terror, humour or despair, have seen and heard one of the most remarkable performances of which the history of English theatrical art can boast.

CHAPTER V.

ADAPTATIONS AND IMPERSONATIONS.

THE immense popularity of the Dickens novels naturally set the stage adaptors to work, and their author, who was always exasperated at the state of the law, which in this respect gives no protection to the novelist, seems to have undergone torments. "Of what he suffered from these adaptations of his books," says Mr. Forster, "multiplied remorselessly at every theatre, I have forborne to speak, but it was the subject of complaint with him incessantly; and more or less satisfied as he was with individual performances, such as Mr. Yates's Quilp or Mantalini, and Mrs. Keeley's Smike or Dot, there was only one, that of Barnaby Rudge by the Miss Fortescue who became afterwards Lady Gardner, on which I ever heard him dwell with a thorough liking." In 1844 he wrote: "I saw the 'Carol' last night" (it was a version done at the Adelphi), "better than usual, and Wright seems to enjoy Bob Cratchit, but *heart-breaking* to me. Oh, Heaven! if any forecast of *this* was ever in my mind! Yet O. Smith was drearily better than

I expected. It is a great comfort to have that kind of meat underdone, and his face is quite perfect." "It is true," Mr. Forster continues, "that to the dramatisations of his next and other following Christmas stories he gave help himself; but even then, all such efforts to assist special representations were mere attempts to render more tolerable what he had no power to prevent, and, with a few rare exceptions, they were never very successful."

This, to the present day, remains more or less true; but it should be added that more recent adaptations have been better executed (notably those that came from the sympathetic pen of the late Andrew Halliday), and that some of them have been decidedly and not undeservedly popular. Dickens smarted under what he, not unnaturally, considered a wrong, and in his criticism he was proportionately severe.

One of the first writers for the stage to turn his attention to the plots and characters created by Dickens, was William Moncrieff, and on July 10th, 1837, his three-act adaptation of "Pickwick," entitled "Sam Weller; or, the Pickwickians," was performed for the first time at the Theatre Royal, Strand. Protests and remonstrances were made, and the printed copy of this work is heralded by the following self-satisfied and fiery "Advertisement."

"It is almost needless to observe, that this drama is founded on the very original, graphic, and clever 'Posthumous Papers of the Pickwick Club,' written by Mr. Dickens, better known through his familiar cognomen 'Boz.' It will be quite supererogatory to point out the numerous instances in which I have been obliged, for the purposes of the stage, to depart from my original, as the Papers are in everybody's hands, and the deviations speak for themselves; it may be sufficient to say, that I have, in no instance, I trust, departed from the spirit of my prototype, however greatly I may have been compelled to vary from their form and bearing; and that I have endeavoured to make the quantity of original matter I was necessitated to write amalgamate, not unworthily, I trust, with the materials borrowed from Mr. Dickens. It would have been a much more easy and genial task for me to have written an entirely original work; especially, labouring as I have been, for some time past, under the calamity of, I hope only temporary, blindness; but I was rather piqued than otherwise to the work. The Papers had been pronounced to be wholly undramatic; two very talented gentlemen, to use a newspaper term, had both attempted the task and failed—the one from sticking too closely to his original, the other through departing too widely from it.

It struck me they were to be *made* dramatic. I knew well their author had never contemplated the production of them in dramatic shape, or he would have formed a regular plot, and given a continuity to his work, which alone is wanting to rank it with the finest comic fictions of any age or country. The success of my undertaking has justified my judgment. Some apology is due to Mr. Dickens, for the liberty taken with him in finishing his work before its time; but the great increase of popularity which it must have received from my putting it on the stage, will, I think, more than excuse a step, to which I was urged, rather by circumstance than desire. Some injudicious friends of Mr. Dickens, among his brethren of the Press (preserve me from such friends say I—of course I do not allude to the manly, fair-dealing, daily Press, to which I am under the greatest obligations), have chosen to display much soreness at the complete manner in which I have triumphed over all the difficulties I had to encounter in my undertaking. Every wretched mongrel can, I am aware, dramatise the 'Pickwick Papers,' now that I have shown them how, by closely copying all I have done; as is the case with a low minor theatre, in the purlieus of London—*once* respectable; but even the original author will admit that he had never contemplated his matter could have been so compressed, and his incidents put in so connected a form, as they assume in 'Sam Weller'!—a character, by the by, which I should think was only an after-conception of its creator, and formed no part of his original projection. Mr. Dickens has, by far, too much genius, to nourish any of the petty feelings evinced by his fostering friends! whose articles, being those of the 'high, intellectual' Sunday-school of criticism, are greatly too genteel and abstruse for every-day reading, but must be kept for Lord's-day examination only! Why these gentry should object to my having dramatised Mr. Dickens, I cannot conceive. Sir Walter Scott, a name, I humbly submit, of sufficient merit to be mentioned in the same page with the writer of the 'Pickwick Club,' always looked upon Mr. Pocock's and Mr. Terry's stage versions of those immortal fictions, 'Rob Roy' and 'Ivanhoe,' rather as a compliment than otherwise; and I had undoubted precedent for what I did in the instance of the first dramatic writer of all time— Shakespeare! who has scarcely a play that is not founded on some previous drama, history, chronicle, popular tale, or story. What then means the twaddle of these 'high intellectuals' in so pathetically condoling with Mr. Dickens, on the penalties he pays for his popularity in being put on the stage? Let these 'high intellectuals' speak to Mr. Dickens's publishers, and they will learn it has rendered them, by increasing their sale, the most fortunate of Chapmen and dealers! It is wasting time to show the absurdity of these addle-pated persons, for their 'blow hot and blow cold' articles are as incomprehensible to themselves as they are to everybody else. In one of them, I am, first of all, abused for having sacrilegiously meddled with any of Mr. Dickens's matter; and then abused for not having meddled with it enough. The reader is told that everybody is pleased with my piece; and is then informed that nobody should be pleased with it. Two or three low scenes between Sam and his father, taken from the original work, are lauded as 'written in a fine spirit of humanity'; while some rather polite dialogues, that I have introduced, between the ladies, are blackguarded by this 'high intellectual' as vulgar."

Much more to the same purpose has the irate adaptor to say before he comes to "the more grateful task" of acknowledging the excellence of the acting of some of those who took part in his much criticised play. "By his impersonation of Sam Weller," he says, "Mr. Hammond has placed himself at the very head of his profession—it is one of the most perfect performances the British stage can now boast of,"—and he has nothing but praise for the Mr. Weller, Sen. of

Mr. H. Hall; the Job Trotter of Mr. Attwood; the Jingle of Mr. Lee; the Mr. Pickwick of Mr. Younge; the Fat Boy (called by Mr. Moncrieff "Master Joseph Dumpling,") of Mr. A. Richardson; the Isabella Wardle of Mrs. Hammond; and the Emily Wardle of Miss Daly.

As a specimen of Mr. Moncrieff's success in " not departing from the spirit of his prototype," it may be mentioned that the last scene of " Sam Weller " shows " London, on the Accession of the Queen," where the " Populace in holiday clothes " listen to some dialogue between Mr. Pickwick and Sam; and then join all the characters in a loyal chorus to the air of " Auber's God Save the King! Gustavus," during the singing of which, a " *Procession of Heralds, Beefeaters, Guards, etc., are seen passing through Temple Bar to proclaim the Accession of Her Majesty, Queen Victoria, and the piece concludes, amidst general shouts of joy and congratulation, with Tableau!* "

Dickens had his " return match " with Moncrieff (who continued to dramatise his works) by introducing the character of the " literary gentleman " to the farewell supper given to Mr. Vincent Crummles, and this was responded to by the thin-skinned adaptor in the following " proclamation : "

NEW STRAND THEATRE.

NICHOLAS NICKLEBY.

To the Public.

SOME of the Newspapers having named me as the person intended to be represented by an intemperate and vulgar caricature in the last published number of NICHOLAS NICKLEBY, which without such information I should certainly never have suspected, it may perhaps be necessary to say a few words in order to set the Public right upon the matter.

Mr. Dickens complains that I have, in the present very successful adaptation of "Nicholas Nickleby," "finished" his "unfinished work," have "anticipated his plot," "which had cost him many thoughtful days and sleepless nights," that I am a *Richard Turpin*, a *Tom King*, and a *Jerry Abershaw* (that is, presuming he really means me). In fact, that I am nothing more or less than a species of Novel Highwayman, an universal Robber of Romance, having dramatised no less than *two hundred and forty-seven Novels*, as fast as they came out, and very often, *Mirabile dictu*, even "faster than they came out," though I know not well how that could be. That

I have stolen his brains (it would certainly appear that he had lost them), an act which he considers equal in turpitude to stealing his pocket-handkerchief, valuing the one at the same rate as the other, and I know not what other atrocities besides. I certainly plead guilty to having dramatised his work, which I should not have done till it had been completed had not two other playwrights dramatised it before me, a circumstance that did not seem displeasing either to Mr. Dickens or his proprietors, Messrs. Chapman & Hall, as the latter themselves actually published one of the adaptations alluded to, and thus made themselves parties to it; independently of which I did not commence my version till the original work had been nearly fifteen months before the Public, and the *dénouement* was obviously in view:—that I should unfortunately have hit upon the same way of ending the history as that projected by Mr. Dickens, and thereby have caused him any annoyance, I really regret; but there is a very easy way of making me " hide my diminished head," let Mr. Dickens—and he has five months before him—set his wits to work again, and finish *his* " Nicholas Nickleby " *better than I have done*, and I shall sink into the primitive mire, from which I have for a moment attempted to emerge by catching at the hem of his garment, a fate I shall deserve for my Quixotic foolhardiness for continuing, as he says, " to drag into the magic circle of my dulness subjects not at all dramatic, cutting, hacking, and carving them to the powers and capacities of my actors and the capabilities of my theatre," and " persuading the innocent Public, night after night, to admire and applaud them." I could wish it were generally agreed that no original Novel, Romance, or Tale should be made use of for dramatic or other purposes, without the original Author having an interest in such appropriation, but as such is not the case, and the works of novelists, &c., have at all times been considered fair game to the Dramatist, without any complaint from their Authors, I do not perceive why I should be expected to become a solitary exception, and be debarred an advantage allowed to all others. I never dramatised but *five* Novels in my life—Mrs. Opie's beautiful " Father and Daughter," Sir Walter Scott's matchless " Ivanhoe," Sir Edward Bulwer's masterly and complete " Eugene Aram," the " Pickwick Miscellany," and, lastly, Mr. Dickens's very clever " Nicholas Nickleby." Had the slightest intimation been conveyed to me, either by Mr. Dickens or his *proprietors*, that my using his work would be disagreeable or inimical, I should immediately have desisted; but the fact is, as in the case of " Sam Weller," had the work been less successfully finished, not a word would have been uttered in depreciation of my using it by Mr. Dickens.

I willingly admit that the common practice of dramatising works before their original authors have completed them, is an unfair and vexatious one; but it did not originate with me. I regret Mr. Dickens should have lost his temper, and descended to scurrility and abuse, where a temperate remonstrance alone was needed, but has suffered his irritability to make him forget the good-breeding of a gentleman, and lose sight of that sense which should ever characterise a man of letters. As one of his admirers, I lament he should so far have committed himself. Mr. Dickens is at perfect liberty, if it will at all gratify his spleen, to call me the veriest blockhead that ever catered for the stage : the Public have too often decided upon my very humble pretensions to be swayed by his *ipse dixit* now. Great as his talents are, he is not to fancy himself "Sir Oracle," and think that when he speaks no dog should " bark "; he should not attempt to "bestride us like a Colossus," and grumble that we "poor petty mortals should seek to creep between his legs." With all possible good feeling, I would beg to hint to Mr. Dickens that the depreciating the talents of another is but a shallow and envious way of attempting to raise one's own—that the calling the offending party a thief, sneering at his pecuniary circumstances, and indulging in empty boasts of tavern treats, are weapons of offence usually resorted to only by the very lowest orders. Nothing is more easy than to be ill-natured. I confess I write for my living, and it is no discredit to Mr. Dickens to say that those who know him best are aware he is as much indebted to his pen for the dinner of the day as I can possibly be. With respect to the "*six hundred generations*" through which Mr. Dickens expects his "pedestal should remain unshaken in the Temple of Fame," I can assure him I have never anticipated that any credit I might derive from dramatising Nicholas Nickleby would more than endure beyond as many days. Having himself *unsuccessfully* tried the Drama, there is some excuse for Mr. Dickens's petulance towards its professors; but it is somewhat illiberal and ungrateful that, being indebted to the stage for so many of his best characters—*Sam Weller*, from Beazley's "Boarding House," for example—he should deny it a few in return. In putting his present Novel upon the stage, there was no intention to injure or annoy him; and if it will be any satisfaction to him, I promise him that whatever offence I may have committed in the present instance shall not be repeated in the future—at least by me.

I cannot avail myself of the liberal offer of

"paying the tavern bill," as a long and severe illness of nearly five years, with its consequent deprivation of sight, has, during almost all that period, wholly prevented my " taking my ease in mine inn," however I might have wished it. And now, hoping that Mr. Dickens may speedily regain his good-humour, and indulge in a little more generosity of feeling towards his humbler brethren of the quill, I cordially bid him farewell.

> "Let the galled jade wince,
> My withers are unwrung."

WILLIAM MONCRIEFF.

June 5th, 1839.

This is not very pretty reading, and it is pleasant to turn to other sides of what, until the existing laws of copyright are altered, must remain a vexed question.

An early and successful stage-adaptor of Dickens's novels was Mr. Edward Stirling, and in his entertaining book entitled "Old Drury Lane," he has some interesting things to say about his work in this direction. "For the Adelphi Company," he writes, "I adapted 'Nicholas Nickleby,' in 1838. It was performed at that theatre for the first time on November 19, 1838. The piece had a long run—one hundred and sixty nights. The following was the cast:

Ralph Nickleby	Cullenford.
Nicholas Nickleby	John Webster.
Newman Noggs	O. Smith.
Mantalini	Yates.
Squeers	Wilkinson.
Scaley	Saunders.
Smike	Mrs. Keeley.
John Browdie	H. Beverly.
Mrs. Nickleby	Miss O'Neil.
Kate Nickleby	Miss Cotteril.
Madame Mantalini	Miss Shaw.
Miss Knagg	Miss George.
Miss Squeers	Miss Gower.
Miss Price	Miss Grove.
Mrs. Squeers	Miss Fosbroke.

Speaking of this performance, Mr. Forster says: "He (Dickens) had been able to sit through Nickleby, and to see a merit in parts of the representation. Mr. Yates had a sufficiently humorous meaning in his wildest extravagance, and Mr. O. Smith could put into his queer angular oddities enough of a hard dry pathos to conjure up shadows at least of Mantalini and Newman Noggs. A quaint actor, named Wilkinson, proved equal to the drollery, though not the fierce brutality, of Squeers; and even Dickens, in the letter telling me of his visit to the theatre, was able to praise 'the skilful management and dressing of the boys, the capital manner and speech of Fanny Squeers, the dramatic representation of her card-party in Squeers's parlour, the careful making up of all the people, and the exceedingly good tableaux formed from Browne's sketches. Mrs. Keeley's first appearance beside the fire, and all the rest of Smike was excellent.'"

A very carefully mounted, and, on the whole, well-cast version of "Nicholas Nickleby," for which Mr. Andrew Halliday was responsible, was produced at the same theatre in 1875. On this occasion those two excellent, and alas! dead and gone comedians, Mr. John Clarke and Mr. George Belmore, were seen at their best as Squeers and Newman Noggs. Mr. Terriss was a capital Nicholas, Mr. S. Emery an acceptable John Browdie; Mr. James Fernandez an impressive Ralph; Mrs. Alfred Mellon a venomous Mrs. Squeers, and Miss Lydia Foote a pathetic Smike. In this adaptation the character of Mantalini was omitted, and a great "realistic" feature was made of the starting of the Yorkshire coach from the "Saracen's Head." In 1885, in what can only be termed a dramatic fragment taken from the book (the adaptor called it an "episodic sketch"), Mr. John S. Clarke, the famous American comedian, gave, at the Strand Theatre, a wonderfully clever impersonation of Newman Noggs. A performance of Mr. Stirling's version at Worthing was not given under the advantages of the one that won some praise from Dickens at the Adelphi. "For my benefit," says Mr. Stirling, "'Nicholas Nickleby' was announced. Without the 'Dotheboys Hall' scholars, this performance could not, however, take place. And here was the awkward dilemma. Worthing mothers of the poorer class did not countenance play-acting, believing old Nick to be in some way connected with it. A local Figaro helped me out of my difficulty. The professor of the razor did a bit of most things at his odd and leisure moments. He was a performer on the French horn, a bird fancier, newsvendor, corn-cutter—Heaven knows what besides—a regular Caleb Quotem, in short. 'I'll get you fifty, sir, never fear.' And he was as good as his word. Lured from the by-streets and alleys by his horn, like the children in the 'Pied Piper of Hamelin,' the small fry followed him to the theatre yard; once there, Figaro closed the gates upon Mr. Squeers's children. Amidst crying and moaning they were placed on the stage, sitting on benches, and kept in order by Figaro's cane—poor children, completely bewildered. When the treacle was administered, most of them cried. This delighted the audience, thinking it so natural (so it was). At nine o'clock, the act over, our cruel barber threw open the gates, driving his flock out, with a pleasant intimation of what they would catch when they arrived home. Mothers, fathers, sisters, in wild disorder, had been scouring the town for their runaways, and the police were completely puzzled and at their wit's ends at such a wholesale kidnapping. Figaro was nearly torn to pieces when the truth was discovered."

The City of London Theatre, built by Mr. Beasly, was opened for the first time, April 27th, 1837, with the original stage adaptation of the "Pickwick Papers," by Mr. Stirling, with the following cast:

Mr. Pickwick	Williams	*(of the Haymarket).*
Sam Weller	Wilkinson	*(Adelphi).*
Fat Boy	Tully	*(the Composer).*
Jingle	Fitzpatrick.	

For obvious reasons, the "Pickwick Papers" will never make a really satisfactory acting play, and yet for the sake of one marvellous impersonation its stage representation will always be welcome and memorable to the playgoers of to-day. Of course we allude to the Jingle of Mr. Henry Irving. This splendid piece of character acting would no doubt have excited the admiration of Dickens himself.

The impudent strolling player is personified to the life, and the creation of Dickens stamped with the hall-mark of the acting genius of Irving is a thing once seen to be ever remembered.

The Serjeant Buzfuz of Mr. Toole, too, will always give popularity to the representation of "Bardell *v.* Pickwick," and at benefit performances brilliant theatrical names are often to be found in the jury-box during the stage hearing of that famous trial. We think it may truly be said that a really satisfactory impersonation of Mr. Pickwick was never seen upon the stage.

Concerning an adaptation of "The Old Curiosity Shop," in which, at the Adelphi, Yates played Quilp, and Mrs. Keeley was the Little Nell, Mr. Stirling quotes the following amusing, and eminently managerial letter:

"DEAR STIRLING,

"Quilp's up in public estimation; Nell's down. I'll keep her there.

"Yours truly,

"F. YATES."

The "Old Curiosity Shop," has always been a favourite subject with the stage adaptor, and some comparatively recent performances of the most strongly drawn among the familiar characters will be pleasantly remembered by the Dickens-loving playgoer. The late John Clarke was a wonderful Quilp. In make-up and in dress, he perfectly realised the well-known illustrations of " Phiz," and the unfortunate lameness which somewhat marred the majority of his later performances, in this part only added to its elfish grotesqueness, and ghoulish power. It was a marvellous reproduction of the combined conception of artist and author. In the same excellent version, which was first produced at the Olympic, George Belmore displayed both force and pathos as the Grandfather—and almost all the characters were satisfactorily played—but it remained for Mr. Frank Wyatt, in a much later adaptation, given at the Opera Comique (when Miss Lotta, the American actress, gave an extravagant impersonation of The Marchioness), to completely realise the humours of Dick Swiveller. A pit-fall to some actresses has been a desire to display versatility of talent by " doubling " the parts of The Marchioness, and Little Nell, and the result has always been disastrous to one or other of the two characters, and sometimes to both. Poor Nell, however, has generally been the greater sufferer.

Mr. Stirling also prepared, for Mr. and Mrs. Keeley, who were then the managers of the Lyceum, the first stage version of Martin Chuzzlewit. With the following cast the piece had a successful run of 280 nights :—

Young Martin Chuzzlewit	F. Vining.
Old Martin Chuzzlewit	R. Younge.
Pecksniff	F. Mathews.
Tigg	Alfred Wigan.
Jonas	Emery.
Tom Pinch	Meadows.
Bailey	Mrs. Keeley.
Mrs. Gamp	Keeley.
Betsy Prig	Collier.
Mrs. Todgers	Mrs. F. Mathews.
Mercy	Miss Woolgar.
Charity	Miss Pincott.

More recent noteworthy assumptions have been the splendidly comic impersonation of Mrs. Gamp by John Clarke (poor Clarke seemed to have taken Dickens in "at the pores"), the capitally realised Pecksniff of Mr. Lionel Brough; and the cleverly touched Tom Pinch of Mr. Thomas Thorne.

The pleasantest thing which Mr. Stirling has to tell with regard to his connection with Dickens is concerning his dramatisation of the "Christmas Carol," which was done by the express sanction of the author. The story is in itself so charming, and is so daintily told, that Mr. Stirling's own words must be used:

"Dickens attended several rehearsals, furnishing valuable suggestions. Thinking to make Tiny Tim (a pretty child) more effective, I ordered a set of irons and bandages for his supposed weak leg. When Dickens saw this tried on the child, he took me aside:

"'No, Stirling, no; this won't do! remember how painful it would be to many of the audience having crippled children.'"

Although it is to be found among the published letters, Mr. Stirling also appropriately records Dickens's written reply to the earnest entreaty of the ladies and gentlemen of the theatrical profession that he would give two or three morning readings that they might have an opportunity of hearing him. It ran as follows:

"Gad's-Hill Place,
"Higham by Rochester, Kent.
"Wednesday, March 24, 1869.

"LADIES AND GENTLEMEN,

"I beg to assure you that I am much gratified by the desire you do me the honour to express in your letter handed to me by Mr. John Clarke.

"Before that letter reached me I had heard of your wish, and had mentioned to Messrs. Chappell that it would be highly agreeable to me to anticipate it if possible. They readily responded, and we agreed upon having three morning readings in London. As they are not yet publicly announced, I add a note of the days and subjects.

"Saturday, May 1st. 'Boots at the Holly-Tree Inn,' and 'Sikes and Nancy,' from 'Oliver Twist.'

"Saturday, May 8th. 'The Christmas Carol.'

"Saturday, May 22nd. 'Sikes and Nancy,' from 'Oliver Twist,' and 'The Trial,' from 'Pickwick.'

"With the warmest interest in your art, and in its claims upon the general gratitude and respect,

"Believe me always
"Faithfully your friend,
"CHARLES DICKENS.

"To the ladies and gentlemen—my correspondents through Mr. Clarke."

The "Sikes and Nancy," scene was notoriously the most dramatic among Dickens's readings, and it is noteworthy that he selected it twice for his dramatic audience.

It is unnecessary to the purpose of these pages to give a complete list of the dramas and farces founded on the novels of Dickens. Those who are interested in the subject cannot do better than refer to the "Dramatic" chapter of Mr. Fred G. Kitton's wonderful book entitled "Dickensiana." Wonderful is really the only word for this most attractive volume. The information gathered together by Mr. Kitton on all matters connected with Dickens and his works, is not only invaluable, but, apparently, exhaustive, and to give a second list would be only to repeat work that has already been thoroughly well done.

Disparagingly as Mr. Forster speaks of these adaptations, and annoying and disappointing as many of them must have been to Dickens, there is no doubt that they were eagerly expected by the playgoing public, and some of the representations were certainly, in a large degree, successful.

For example, in January, 1846, in that capital but short-lived little periodical, " The Almanack of the Month," a critic who signs himself " W. H. W." thus speaks of the first performance of a stage version of " The Cricket on the Hearth," at the Lyceum :

" That the Cricket might be served up quite warm to the playgoing public, on the *foyer* of the Lyceum Theatre, its author—Mr. Charles Dickens —supplied the dramatist, Mr. Albert Smith, with proof-sheets hot from the press. On the evening of the morning, therefore, on which the book was published, its dramatic version was produced; and, as the adaptor stuck very closely indeed to the text of the original, of course it succeeded. Why, we are going to explain.

" Although Mr. Dickens does not profess dramatic authorship, yet his writings have had a considerable influence on the stage. The characters in his novels are—despite the exaggeration with which a few of the critical fraternity charge him—completely natural; so essentially natural, indeed, that even after some of the stage adaptors and actors have done their worst upon them, they come upon the stage very like transcripts from real life. As plays they are altogether different from their predecessors. The *dramatis personæ* cannot, as that of the sentimental comedy and heavy melodrama, be summarily and arbitrarily put into the various conventional classes amongst which stage managers distribute the 'parts.' One cannot safely be given out at once to the 'heavy father' of the company; another to the 'smart servant'; a third to the 'low comedian'; a fourth to the 'juvenile tragedian'; a fifth to the 'chambermaid,' or a sixth to the 'sentimental young lady.' Dickens's characters are too like nature for that. No individual is, in real life, always being funny, or behaving wickedly, or eternally breathing forth sentimentality. The same persons have their times for being gay, and for being sad; they have their times for being brilliant and their dull moments; and so have the life portraits which Dickens draws. Some dramatists have attempted to set "Boz's" compositions 'to rights' for the stage, and to make his characters stagily 'effective' after their own tastes, and the consequence has been that plays done on that principle have been as unnatural as a pantomime. In the present instance, the dramatist has stuck to his text."

Speaking of the performance, he says:

"Mr. Keeley, without any regard to his usual 'line' of character, was grave and comic by turns. He played Caleb Plummer, the toy maker. Mr. Emery, the carter, acted and dressed as like a carrier as if he had walked straight from the yard of the 'Blossoms Inn,' or had been suddenly transplanted from the 'Flower Pot.' Mr. Meadows, the master toyman, was as like an evil genius as a man in plum-coloured clothes and gaiters could be; and Mr. F. Vining pretended to be deaf with a degree of success which at first nearly took us in; and afterwards to be a young lover, with all the agility and sprightliness as he displayed at that time immemorial when he first took to the juvenile line of business. Slowboy was said on the bills to be a Miss Turner, but so life-like was her acting, that we could hardly dissuade ourselves from the notion that she was "Boz's" genuine and particular Slowboy, clothed and animated. The young lady who performed the fairy of the fireplace also deserves a word or praise. She came up through the hearth, and spoke a long speech just before the bars of a tolerably severe fire without wincing."

. The critic closes his remarks with expressions of unstinted admiration for the Dot of Mrs. Keeley, a performance which was at the time generally acknowledged to be one of the most perfect in that delightful actress's extensive repertory. Mr. and Mrs. Keeley, indeed, were amongst the first, the greatest, and the best of the impersonators of Dickens's characters.

It must, however, be owned that some very extraordinary and exasperating stage adaptations of Dickens's works have from time to time been written and performed. Take, for example, the " Oliver Twist," of Mr. George Almar, which was produced at the Surrey Theatre, November 19th, 1838, and which, at the price of one penny, and with the announcement of " This Play can be performed without risk of infringing any rights," was published among Dicks' Standard Plays. To show the spirit in which the story is handled, it is only necessary to quote the concluding lines of Mr. Almar's work in which the youthful Oliver (personated by a Master Owen) was absolutely made to *say* the beautiful lines about his unhappy mother with which the novel ends.

" *Mr. Brownlow.* And what is now wanted to complete the happiness of Oliver Twist ? "

" *Oliver.* First that you will erect a small white tablet in the church near which my poor mother died, and on it grave the name of Agnes.

There might be no coffin in that tomb; but if the spirits of the dead ever come back to earth to visit spots hallowed by their love, I do believe that the shade of my poor mother will often hover about this solemn nook, though it is a church, and she was weak and erring."

"*Mr. Brownlow.* The next request I will make for you, dear Oliver, myself, and will make it here—to you (*to audience*) Our hero is but young; but if his simple progress has beguiled you of a smile, or his sorrows of a tear, forgive the errors of the orphan boy, Oliver Twist."

Tableau. *   (See page 185.)

By the way, in speaking of "Oliver Twist," it should not be forgotten that Master Charles Bates at least once made a pointed allusion to things theatrical.

"I never see such a jolly dog as that," cried Master Bates (alluding to the unfortunate animal of which Mr. Sikes was the owner), "Smelling the grub like a old lady a-going to market! He'd make his fortune on the stage that dog would, and rewive the drayma besides."

And it must also be remembered that it was at this very representation of "Oliver Twist" at the Surrey Theatre, in 1838, that Dickens is said to have laid himself down in a corner of the box, and to have risen again only when the curtain had fallen. Macready's diary tells that about this time an adaptation of "Oliver Twist," endorsed with the author's name, was proposed to him, but the actor considered it impracticable for any dramatic purpose.

"Fraser's Magazine" for March, 1842, contains a most amusing account, from the pen of no less a writer than Thackeray, of a performance of a stage version of "Nicholas Nickleby," given in Paris at the Ambigu-Comique Théâtre. Before dealing with the French play, a word of tribute is given to the actors in the English version, which will not be out of place here.

"Who does not remember the pathetic acting of Mrs. Keeley in the part of Smike, as performed at the Adelphi; the obstinate good-humour of Mr. Wilkinson, who, having to represent the brutal Squeers, was, according to his nature, so chuckling, oily, and kind-hearted, that little boys must have thought it a good joke to be flogged by him; finally, the acting of the admirable Yates in the kindred part of Mantalini? Can France, I thought, produce a fop equal to Yates? Is there any vulgarity and assurance in the Boulevard that can be compared to that of which, in the character of Mantalini, he gives a copy so wonderfully close to nature?"

The French play contained many glaring, not to say outrageous, excrescences, and the departures from the story as told by Dickens would be inexcusable if they were not, as told by Thackeray, so intensely amusing. They must be briefly dealt with here :

The scene of the first act was laid in the court of a school, with great iron bars in front, and a beauteous sylvan landscape beyond. The school was known as the "Paradis des Enfans," kept by Mr. Squeers, and in the neighbourhood was supposed to stand the castle of the stately "Earl of Clarendon." Lord Clarendon's daughter takes French lessons from Mr. Squeers' *sous-maitre*, Neekolass Neeklbee, who is, however, no vulgar usher, but lately an orphan; and his uncle, the rich London banker, Monsieur Ralph, taking charge of the lad's portionless sister, has procured for Nicholas the place of usher at a school in "le Yorksheer."

"A rich London banker," exclaims Thackeray, "procuring his nephew a place in a school at eight guineas per annum! Sure there must be some roguery in this; and the more so when you know that Monsieur Squeers, the keeper of the Academy, was, a few years since, a vulgar ropedancer and tumbler at a fair."

While Nicholas is instructing, and it is to be feared making love, to "Meess Annabel," one of Mr. Squeers' scholars, a lad beautifully dressed, fat, clean, and rosy, is in the court-yard receiving lessons *on the clarionet* from John Browdie, who is described as a "drover." This boy is facetiously called by his master "Prospectus," because he is so excessively fat and healthy, and well clothed, that his mere appearance in the court-yard is supposed to entice parents and guardians to place their children in a seminary where the scholars were in such admirable condition. And now Smike (pronounced Smeek) is introduced, and it is explained that ten years since he was left at the "Paradis des Enfans," by a man named Becher, and that since that time he has had no friend except the *sous-maitre* Neeklbee. So the story goes on. Nicholas has his difference with Browdie (concerning "Meess Jenny," the *fermier's* daughter). Browdie, in dudgeon, takes up his stick and sets off to London with a drove of oxen (!),—Nicholas in defence of "Smeek" thrashes Squeers, and the pupils of the Infants' Paradise break bounds and leave their school for ever. The second act is laid in "The tavern of Les Armes du Roi," in London.

"It must be in the Yorkshire Road, that is clear," says Thackeray, "for the first person whom we see there is John Browdie; to him presently comes Prospectus, then Neeklbee, then poor Smeek, each running away individually from the Paradis des Enfans."

"It is likewise at this tavern that the great

banker Ralph does his business, and lets you into a number of his secrets. Hither, too, comes Milor Clarendon, a handsome peer, forsooth, but a sad reprobate I fear. Sorrow has driven him to these wretched courses; ten years since he lost a son, a lovely child of six years of age; and hardened by the loss he has taken to gambling, to the use of the *vins de France*, which take the reason prisoner, and lead to other excitements still more criminal. He has cast his eyes upon the lovely Kate Nickleby (he, the father of Miss Annabel!) and asks the banker to sup with him, to lend him ten thousand pounds, and to bring his niece with him. With every one of these requests the capitalist promises to comply; the money he produces forthwith, the lady he goes to fetch. Ah! milor, beware! beware! your health is bad, your property is ruined, death and insolvency stare you in the face; but what cares Lord Clarendon? He is desperate; he orders a splendid repast in a private apartment, and while they are getting it ready, he and the young lords of his acquaintance sit down and crack a bottle in the coffee-room. A gallant set of gentlemen truly, all in short coats with capes to them, in tights and Hessian boots, such as our nobility are in the custom of wearing.

"'I bet you cinq cents guinées, Lor Beef,' says Milor Clarendon (whom the wine has begun to excite), 'that I will have the lovely Kate Nicklbee at supper with us to-night.'

"'Done!' says Lor Beef. But why starts yon stranger who has just come into the hotel? Why, forsooth? Because he is Nicholas Nickleby, Kate's brother; and a pretty noise he makes when he hears of his lordship's project.

"'You have Meess Neeklebee at your table, sir? You are a liar!'

"All the lords start up.

"'Who is this very strange person?' says Milor Clarendon, as cool as a cucumber.

"'Dog! give me your name!' shouts Nicholas.

"'Ha! ha! ha!' says my lord scornfully.

"'John,' says Nickleby, seizing hold of a waiter, 'tell me that man's name.'

"John the waiter looks frightened, and hums and has, when, at the moment, who should walk in but Mr. Ralph the banker and his niece.

"*Ralph.* 'Nicholas! confusion!'

"*Kate.* 'My brother!'

"*Nicholas.* 'Avaunt, woman! Tell me, sirrah, by what right you bring my sister into such company, and whom is the villain to whom you have presented her?'

"*Ralph.* 'Lord Clarendon.'

"*Nicholas.* 'The father of Meess Annabel? Gracious Heaven!'"

And in this spirit the outrageous travesty (it was worth doing, by the way, if only for the sake of the characteristic wood-cuts with which Thackeray illustrates this article) runs on, until "Smeek" having been discovered to be the heir to the Clarendon estates, is hidden in the "Cadgers' Cavern," a thousand feet below the Thames, is *buried alive!* is rescued by Nicholas and John Browdie, and ultimately becomes Lord Smike; his newly-found sister Annabel openly declaring that, she cares not for rank or fame, the name she loving before all others being that of "Lady Annabel Nickleby."

The article from which these quotations have been made is luckily accessible, and should be read in full by all who appreciate the humour of Dickens, the satire of Thackeray, and the one great author's appreciation of the work of the other.

Acknowledged adaptations of Dickens will certainly continue to be written and produced on the stage for many and many a long year to come; but who shall say how many successful plays have been "suggested" and made popular by his books? In his "Dickensiana" Mr. Kitten deals with this question, and says: "Who, for example, would imagine that the main feature of the plot of Mr. Herman's drama of 'Claudian,' recently performed in London, was suggested by an incident in one of Dickens's Christmas books? Who would have associated such gorgeously-depicted scenes in the life of an emperor with the simple and unaffected story of Christian charity and repentance? Yet such is the case; for Mr. Herman thus relates how he obtained the more beautiful and more pathetic portion of his conception of the hero of the drama. He had found the idea of Claudian's eternal youth and had connected it with the first glimpse of the great curse. He felt that the idea was fine, that it was dramatic; but it was hard and unsympathetic. He had been walking in his garden, it was a brilliant, hot summer day, and to get into complete shade for a while he went into his library. Mechanically his fingers wandered over the shelves, and quite by accident, he took out 'The Christmas Carol' and opened it. His attention was arrested by the little incident in Marley's visit to Scrooge—an incident barely referred to—of the ghost of the fat alderman, who floats about the air with his great chain of ledgers and cash boxes, and who cries bitterly because he cannot relieve the wants of a poor woman who is sitting in the snow on the pavement. In a second Mr. Herman's conception of Claudian is complete. The pathos of a man who desired to do good, and could not do so, gave birth to the idea of the man, every one of whose charitable actions turned to bane, as a punishment for his past crimes. From the ghost of the fat alderman to Claudian is a long distance; but human pathos and passion were the same fifteen hundred years ago as now, and the true poetry of a story, especially its true dramatic poetry, is oftener in the treatment of an idea than in the actual idea itself."

In this way, and often, it may be, without the playwright, who believes himself to be original, knowing that he is something of an adaptor, the characters of Dickens and the episodes in his books find their way on to the stage, and the all-wise playgoer, who is fond of saying that Dickens was no dramatist, is unconsciously indebted to him for his entertainment.

In the year 1852, Mr. Forster tells us, Dickens made a pilgrimage to Walworth, " to see a youth rehearse who was supposed to have talents for the stage, and he was able to gladden Mr. Toole's friends by thinking favourably of his chances of success. 'I remember what I once myself wanted in that way,' he said, ' and I should like to serve him.'"

That Dickens's judgment was not at fault everyone knows, and it is curious to note that the early encouragement of the great novelist acted as an incentive to one of the best and most successful of the stage delineators of his creations.

Of the stage impersonators of Dickens's characters, the genial and popular J. L. Toole takes (who will grudge it him?) first place, and he has many interesting things to tell of his experience in these parts.

When the "Christmas Carol" was played at the Adelphi, with Toole as Bob Cratchit, much realism was got out of the Cratchit Christmas dinner scene, a real roast goose and a real plum-pudding being served up hot every night. Tiny Tim was played by a somewhat emaciated little girl, who sat by the fire-side and was fed with dainty morsels by the other little Cratchits, who clustered about the dinner-table, and who, needless to say, were as willing to play as good a knife and fork on the stage as they are supposed to do in the book.

Of all the little Cratchits, however, this Tiny Tim proved the most voracious. Like his famous young relative Oliver Twist, he always wanted "more," and night after night such large portions of goose and plum-pudding were handed to this exacting and hungry little invalid, that even the good-natured Toole grew annoyed, feeling that the poetry of the scene was being missed, and at last became absolutely angry with the child for its supposed gluttony. Being at length taken to task on the subject, poor Tim made a confession. The child had a sister (a not too well-fed sister) employed in the theatre. The fire by which it sat was a "stage fire," through which anything could be easily conveyed to one waiting on the other side, and poor little Tim's goose and pudding were more than shared each night. When Toole told this story to Dickens he was greatly touched, and said: "I hope you gave the child the whole goose."

Once, when Toole was playing his famous part of Caleb Plummer, in "The Cricket on the Hearth," the actress who was to play the part of the blind girl, Bertha, was suddenly taken ill, and unable to appear; but the stage-manager was equal to the occasion, and sent on another young lady *to read her part!!!*

By-the-way, in addition to Bob Cratchit and Caleb Plummer, Mr. Toole has successfully appeared in stage versions of all the five important Christmas books. As Toby Veck, in "The Chimes" (a pathetic and admirable performance), as Ben Britain, in "The Battle of Life" and as Tetterby, in "The Haunted Man."

Dickens, we need hardly say, duly recognised and admired the matured talents of the comedian whose amateur efforts had secured his critical approbation. He was especially anxious that he should play Joe Gargery, in an adaptation of "Great Expectations" (a part that ultimately fell into the capable hands of Mr.

MR J. L. TOOLE AS "THE ARTFUL DODGER"

Edward Righton), and after seeing and praising his excellent acting as Dick Dolland, in H. J. Byron's "Uncle Dick's Darling," good-humouredly asked if he thought it possible that the dramatist had ever heard of another warm-hearted "cheap-jack" whose name was Dr. Marigold?

One of the best of all Mr. Toole's assumptions is that of the "Artful Dodger." Here Dickens's splendidly drawn character is reproduced to the very life, a fact which has been as heartily recognised by American as by English audiences. Mr. Toole thoroughly realises both the humour and the pathos of Dickens, and never exaggerating either the one or the other, not only pleases the multitude, but gives satisfaction to the most fastidious.

This chapter will hardly be complete without a glance being taken at the successful efforts of other well-known Dickens impersonators. Mr. John Billington, who was the original Ned Plummer in Mr. Boucicault's dramatised version of "The Cricket on the Hearth," has made the part of John Perrybingle his own, playing it with a rough power and pathos that never fails to secure the attention and sympathy of his audiences. In country theatres this impersonation is exceedingly popular. Mr. Billington was, too, the original Walter Wilding, in "No Thoroughfare," when Mrs. Billington played the "Veiled Lady;" Mrs. Alfred Mellon was the delightful Sally Goldstraw; Mr. Henry Neville the manly Vendale; the late Mr. Belmore the lawyer, Mr. Bintry; and the late Mr. Benjamin Webster, in a part somewhat removed from his usual line, the excellent and amusing Joey Ladle. Of Mr. Fechter's vigorous acting as Obenreizer, in this successful play mention has been made elsewhere. It is some eleven years ago since, at the Court Theatre, in Mr. W. S. Gilbert's adaptation of "Great Expectations," Mr. John Clayton excited admiration by his wonderful make-up and acting as the lawyer, Jaggers. This was another portrait that seemed to have stepped out of the novel on to the stage. Later, Mr. Clayton made his greatest success in a character which, though it went under the name of Hugh Trevor, was certainly no other than that of Sidney Carton. Messrs. J. Palgrave Simpson and Herman Merivale, the authors of "All for Her," did not announce their play as an adaptation of "The Tale of Two Cities," nor were they called upon to do so, but they made admirable use of the Carton episodes, and in so doing produced a work which was ungrudgingly acknowledged to be the most powerful that had been seen on the English stage for some years. Speaking of Mr. Clayton's performance in it a critic said: "It does not often fall to the lot of an actor to have such a part as that of Hugh Trevor assigned to him; but, on the other hand, it is not everyone who can grasp his opportunity when it is before him. This Mr. Clayton has done. It would have been easy to make Trevor, the poor, reckless, good-for-nothing drunkard, a very repulsive person; but this Mr. Clayton has not done. Drunk or sober the man is still a gentleman, and from first to last this fact is kept before us with exceptional art." The character of Micawber has naturally been a popular one with comedians. It has been successfully played by Mr. Edward Terry (oddly enough this has so far been the only Dickens part with which the name of that popular actor is associated), Mr. Charles Collette, Mr. David Fisher, Mr. Fernandez, the late Mr. Joseph Eldred, and others; but probably its most successful representative has been found in the American actor, Mr. Rowe. "Mr. Rowe's Micawber," says Mr. Percy Fitzgerald, "is a most enjoyable performance; the player seems to revel in the unctuous platitudes and stick-flourishings—the fitful changes from hopeless despondency born of 'pecuniary embarrassment from his cradle upwards'—to pleasant and eager spirits, on the mention of Punch; his strange and original attitudes, and quaint gamut of tones, make up a very quaint and racy picture. All these oddities of speech and attitude give the notion that they are the honest expression of what is within. Had Mr. Dickens's Micawber never been written, this stage character would have been a very original performance, but it shows what a vast dramatic force lies in all Mr. Dickens's characters."

Mr. Rowe's acting had much to do with the undoubted success that attended the production of Mr. Andrew Halliday's adaptation of " David Copperfield," called " Little Em'ly." The excellence of Miss Ernstone in the character of Martha on this occasion attracted the notice of Dickens himself, and he personally expressed his appreciation of it. The name of Mr. Samuel Emery will always be happily remembered in association with the characters of Dickens. Mr. Emery was the original Jonas Chuzzlewit, Will Fern, and John Perrybingle, and in more recent days his realisation of the character of Dan'l Peggotty was beyond reproach. Of his Captain Cuttle in " Heart's Delight," Mr. Halliday's version of " Dombey and Son," a critic said, " When Mr. Emery comes rolling on to the stage, made up to the very life after the pictures by ' Phiz,' with the rubicund face and the bald pate, the coarse canvas open shirt, and the hook instead of a right hand, the roar that greets the favourite shows that half the actor's work is over. He looks the part, and there is no prejudice on that account." Fortunately, however, Mr. Emery's acting was as good as his make-up, and the pathetic as well as the humourous side of the glorious old " Cap'n " was in his hands depicted to the life.

Referring to the American comedian, Mr. Florence's performance of Captain Cuttle, *Mr. Punch*, under date December 11th, 1880, pithily says—

"' Dombey and Son' was reduced to Florence, Florence appeared as Captain Cuttle twice, and has now disappeared altogether. . . . . As Cuttle he was very funny; he was the well-known pictorial Cuttle down to the ground, and so Phiz-ically he was Cuttle, but morally he was not, unless Americans interpret Charles Dickens's characters after a fashion which is as unintelligible to us as, we venture to say, it would have been to the author. However, in this compressed American tinned essence of 'Dombey and Son,' Captain Cuttle being all Florence, does not even a 'little Paul' on the audience."

The same eminent authority speaking of the adaptation (entitled " Tom Pinch ") of " Martin Chuzzlewit," produced at the Vaudeville in the early months of 1881, says, " Those who have seen ' Tom Pinch ' at the Vaudeville will readily understand why, as a rule, the late Charles Dickens so strongly objected to the dramatisation of his novels. The piece now playing under this title, might just as well have been called ' Tom Anybody '—say ' Tom All-alone.' The stage is said to hold up the mirror to Nature ; in this case the glass used has been of rather inferior quality. The result is a somewhat distorted reflection of an episode in ' Martin Chuzzlewit.' Mr. Tom Thorne appears in the bills as Mr. Tom Pinch, but, in spite of a wig of very peculiar construction, his identity is not altogether lost in his new character, which is not at all the real article, but Pinch-beck. The Pecksniff of Mr. William Farren is sketchily suggestive of Sir Peter Teazle in modern costume ; and the representatives of Cherry and Merry, conscientiously preserve that reputation for burlesque which the Vaudeville enjoyed in the early days of its management——"

"From a snuff-box point of view, this single Pinch is nearly equal to a full mull." Mr. Thorne's Tom Pinch was, nevertheless, an impersonation of much merit.

Mrs. Keeley, the original Dot, and the admirable " creatress " of many other Dickens parts, was especially happy in the character of Clemency Newcome. " The part," said the *Athenæum* of December 26, 1846, " was the life, the soul, the salvation of

MISS JENNIE LEE AS 'JO'.

the new drama. The actress was unwearied by her exertions. Her costume was picturesque, her action and by-play were everywhere appropriate, her tones were full of feeling, honesty, and earnestness. There was the eccentric, hardworking, faithful little body,—an unmistakable identity." In the same part sprightly Miss "Nelly" Farren has also done good service, and the name of this excellent and appreciative actress is also honourably identified with the humours of Tilly Slowboy and Sam Weller, and the delicately portrayed sorrows of poor Smike. Mrs. Jane Stephens, who is generally allowed to be one of the best actresses of what are technically known as "old women's parts" ever known on the English stage, has been seen as a wonderfully artistic, and absolutely uncompromising Mrs. Squeers.

No more deservedly successful Dickens impersonation has been seen than that of the world-wide known Jo, of Miss Jennie Lee. When, in 1876, she played the part for the first time in London, it was rightly said that a more striking revelation of talent had seldom been made. Miss Lee indeed plays Jo with "a realism and a pathos difficult to surpass." "In get-up and in acting," said the *Athenæum*, " the character was thoroughly realised; and the hoarse voice, the slouching, dejected gait, and

12*

the movement as of some hunted animal, were admirably exhibited." Miss Lee's Jo has since won the admiration of audiences, not only throughout the United Kingdom, but in America and Australia, and its popularity remains unabated. In speaking of the adaptation of "Bleak House," in which Miss Lee won fame and fortune, a word of tribute should be paid to the excellence of the Hortense of Miss Dolores Drummond, and the clever portrait of Inspector Bucket, given by Mr. Burnett. Mr. Edward Compton has also done well in this part.

Some of our best comedians have appeared in Dickens's comic female characters. The late Mr. J. Clarke was, as has already been said, a wonderful Mrs. Gamp, and Mr. Lionel Brough has distinguished himself as Tilly Slowboy.

Speaking of Miss Charlotte Cushman in his "Actor's Note Book," Mr. George Vandenhoff says:

"The power of her scorn, and the terrible earnestness of her revenge were immense. Her greatest part, fearfully natural, dreadfully intense, horribly real, was Nancy Sikes, in the dramatic version of 'Oliver Twist'; it was too true, it was painful, this actual presentation of Dickens's poor abandoned, abused, murdered, outcast of the streets; a tigress with the touch, and but one, of woman's almost deadened nature, blotted and trampled under foot by man's cruelty and sin." Nancy has been a favourite part with other actresses, and Mr. Lionel Brough, who, when he so wills it, never fails to make his hearers laugh, has absolutely terrified them with the wild force of his admirably conceived and conscientiously portrayed, Bill Sikes. It is satisfactory to know that in his recent brilliant series of revivals of Lyceum triumphs, Mr. Henry Irving has not forgotten the success that he made in earlier days in the character of Jingle, and it is pleasant to see that the gifted actor-manager, who has made an undoubtedly great name in the highest branches of the drama, is still alive to the importance and high-standing of the art of the character delineator or eccentric comedian. Mr. Irving's very acceptable decision to reappear as Jingle, at a time when he is acknowledged to be the best Hamlet and the finest Shylock of his day, has been amply justified by the enthusiasm with which the impersonation has been received. At the Lyceum, the adaptation of "Pickwick" has very wisely been narrowed to the dimensions of a farce, with Jingle for its central figure. "Mr. Irving," says a critic, "disdains none of the acts of the low comedian. He vaults lightly over the back of Mr. Archer, who represents Job Trotter, and he even turns his back to the audience, and with his hands in his coat-tail pockets, betrays the fact that he has been sitting somewhere upon fresh paint or whitewash. It must not be supposed, however, that it is by these to tell the truth, rather unworthy arts alone that he is enabled to cause hearty amusement. It is sufficient to refer, in proof of this assertion, to the scene in which Jingle bamboozles poor Mr. Pickwick, whom he knows to be listening, by shedding sympathetic tears as he entertains Job Trotter with a recital of his beloved mother's distresses. Mr. Albery's adaptation in its present condensed form, is very properly styled a farce, but this particular scene is comedy, and comedy of a high order, and it is finely played by Mr. Irving, whose whole speech and bearing have in them the very quintessence of hypocrisy."

Of Mr. Irving's first appearance as Jingle, a critic truthfully said : " Mr. Irving imparted to the character a strange flavour of originality, movement, and grotesque vivacity. The face assumed an intelligent leanness, a Callot-like intelligence and oddity. But there was much more. This vivacity is not in life confined to pattering over words glibly. An adventurer of the kind must be restlessly watching faces and movements of figures, and this will impart a certain spasmodic nervousness. Mr. Irving's figure seemed to acquire this. His shoulders went up towards his ears, his shoulder-blades worked, his talk was strange and flourishing. These were no unmeaning antics, but a nice instinct had shown him that they were appropriate—that a man of such pursuits would necessarily by his over-eagerness and anxiety, make such movements. Even to the little traditional tricks of the stage, he gives an originality; as when he puts the watch by mistake into his pocket, it had the air of a mistake; but how often have we seen the 'funny' man do the same with an elaborate ostentation, taking the audience into his confidence with nods and winks?"

In the latest Lyceum stage edition of "Pickwick," the veteran, and always excellent Mr. Howe, succeeding the late Mr. Addison as Mr. Pickwick, at least contrived to look the part to the life, and Mr. Stephen Caffery was a very satisfactory Sam Weller. It is curious to note that while many of our best actors have done well in Dickens's characters, comparatively few actresses have made in them more than passing successes. It is true that Mrs. Kendal, undoubtedly the greatest actress of the day, has played Bertha in "The Cricket on the Hearth," with all the delightful tenderness of touch and subtlety of art of which she is the mistress; but the part is by no means what is styled a "great" one, and it must be admitted that what, in theatrical parlance would be called the "leading characters" in Dickens's novels, do not lend themselves so well to stage purposes as his humorous and "cabinet" portraits.

Mr. Percy Fitzgerald thoroughly understood this when, in his "Principles of Comedy and Dramatic Effect," speaking of "Little Em'ly" at the Olympic, he said : " One of the charms of Mr. Dickens's humour are those sudden analogies between objects of mind and matter—strange and surprising likenesses — and which is indeed opening a new world. Another feature lies not so much in making the characters, as in ' bringing them out ' by the curious comments, hints, and remarks of the novelist himself. It is as though we were witnessing all the scenes of the story, with a mysterious spirit by our side, who had privileged and Asmodean access to secret interiors of house and mind. Thus is given, for behaviour and speech and deportment, otherwise unmeaning, a secret key, which makes all intelligible. Now it is obvious that on the stage all this must be lost. Numbers who go to the Olympic see David Copperfield himself on the boards, in a strange coat and gilt buttons, follow him as he moves amongst the other characters, and would own that he fulfils his duty to the play respectably. He has about the same business that he has in the story—friend of Steerforth and Peggotty, unmasker of Uriah Heep, and so forth. Given that selection of episodes now being played, it might be asked, What more could be added to the part? Yet this is a superficial view. Turn to the story, and we find that his is the mind which reflects and colours the whole course of events to us. Through him, as it were, we see every character; it is his mind, his feeling, the mind of the author himself, and his own life, that fills up the whole. Through the eyes of David, look forth the eyes of the writer; his quick wit, his genius, illuminates that figure, brings out the wit and humour of others, as steel does with flint, and illustrates their doings with a sort of commentary. Thus Copperfield becomes the soul of all. We turn to the stage, and all this must disappear; there remains but a figure in a long coat and gilt buttons, who walks on and walks off, and is about as purposeless as one of Madame Tussaud's images. Not but that the adaptor has done his part with a surprising tact and self-abnegation; and we only use his skilful adaptation to illustrate a principle."

* Note to page 162.—The writer has seen a stage-version of "Little Dorrit" in which the Father of the Marshalsea inherits a title, and is hailed as Sir William Dorrit: and an adaptation of "Dombey and Son" in which poor Paul is stolen by Mrs. Brown, and meets with his death while endeavouring to escape, by way of the roof, from that good lady's house!

CHAPTER VI.

THE STAGE IN HIS SPEECHES.

As the following extracts will prove, Charles Dickens's interest in, and knowledge of, everything connected with the theatre were nowhere better shown than in his public speeches.

On June 27th, 1855, speaking in Drury Lane Theatre on the subject of Administrative Reform, he made the following happy allusions to his surroundings in referring to the term, "the private theatricals at Drury Lane," which had been applied to the proceedings in question:

"Now, I have some slight acquaintance with theatricals, private and public, and I will accept that figure of the noble lord. I will not say that if I wanted to form a company of Her Majesty's servants, I think I know where to put my hand on 'the comic old gentleman'; nor that, if I wanted to get up a pantomime, I fancy I know what establishment to go to for the tricks and changes, also for a very considerable host of supernumeraries, to trip one another up in that contention with which many of us are familiar, both on these and on other boards, in which the principal objects thrown about are loaves and fishes. But I will try to give the noble lord the reason for these private theatricals, and the reason why, however ardently he may desire to ring the curtain down upon them, there is not the faintest present hope of their coming to a conclusion. It is this: the public theatricals which the noble lord is so condescending as to manage are so intolerably bad, the machinery is so cumbrous, the parts so ill-distributed, the company so full of 'walking-gentlemen,' the managers have such large families, and are so bent on putting those families into what is theatrically called 'first business'—not because of their aptitude for it, but because they *are* their families—that we find ourselves bound to organise an opposition. We have seen the *Comedy of Errors* played so dismally like a tragedy that we really cannot bear it. We are, therefore, making bold to get up the *School of Reform*, and we hope, before the play is out, to improve that noble lord by our performance very considerably. If he object that we have no right to improve him without his license, we venture to claim that right in virtue of his orchestra, consisting of a very powerful piper, whom we always pay."

On July 21st, 1858, he spoke at a public meeting held at the Princess's Theatre, for the purpose of establishing the Royal Dramatic College. Mr. Charles Kean (who was at the time appearing in his memorable revival of "The Merchant of Venice,"), occupied the chair, and in the course of his remarks, Dickens said:

"I could not but reflect, whilst Mr. Kean was speaking, that in an hour or two from this time, the spot upon which we are now assembled will be transformed into the scene of a crafty and a cruel bond. I know that, a few hours hence, the Grand Canal of Venice will flow, with picturesque fidelity, on the very spot where I now stand dryshod, and that 'the quality of mercy' will be beautifully stated to the Venetian Council by a learned young doctor from Padua, on these very boards on which we now enlarge upon the quality of charity and sympathy. Knowing this, it came into my mind to consider how different the real bond of to-day is from the ideal bond of to-night. Now, all generosity, all forbearance, all forgetfulness of little jealousies and unworthy divisions, all united action for the general good. Then, all selfishness, all malignity, all cruelty, all revenge, and all evil—now all good. Then, a bond to be broken within the compass of a few—three or four—swiftly-passing hours;—now, a bond to be valid and of good effect generations hence."

On May 11th, 1864, at a meeting held at the

Adelphi Theatre for the purpose of founding the Shakespeare Schools, in connection with the Royal Dramatic College, he said :

"Broadly, ladies and gentlemen, this is the whole design. There are foundation scholars at Eton, foundation scholars at nearly all our old schools, and if the public, in remembrance of a noble part of our standard national literature, and in remembrance of a great humanising art, will do this thing for these children, it will at the same time be doing a wise and good thing for itself, and will unquestionably find its account in it. Taking this view of the case—and I cannot be satisfied to take a lower one—I cannot make a sorry face about "the poor player." I think it is a term very much misused and very little understood—being, I venture to say, appropriated in a wrong sense by players themselves. Therefore, ladies and gentlemen, I can only present the player to you exceptionally in this wise—that he follows a peculiar and precarious vocation, a vocation very rarely affording the means of accumulating money—that that vocation must, from the nature of things, have in it many undistinguished men and women to one distinguished one, that it is not a vocation the exerciser of which can profit by the labours of others, but in which he must earn every loaf of his bread in his own person, with the aid of his own face, his own limbs, his own voice, his own memory, and his own life and spirits; and these failing, he fails. Surely this is reason enough to render him some little help in opening for his children their paths through life. I say their paths advisedly, because it is not often found, except under the pressure of necessity, or where there is strong hereditary talent—which is always an exceptional case—that the children of actors and actresses take to the stage. Persons therefore need not in the least fear that by helping to endow these schools they would help to overstock the dramatic market. They would do directly the reverse, for they would divert into channels of public distinction and usefulness those good qualities which would otherwise languish in that market's over-rich superabundance."

* * * * *

"It has happened in these later times that objections have been made to children of dramatic artists in certain little snivelling private schools—but in public schools never. Therefore, I hold that the actors are wise, and gratefully wise, in recognising the capacious liberality of a public school, in seeking not a little hole-and-corner place of education for their children exclusively, but in addressing the whole of the great middle class, and proposing to them to come and join them, the actors, in their own property, in a public school, in a part of the country where no such advantage is now to be found."

On February 14th, 1866, Dickens officiated as chairman at the annual dinner of the Dramatic, Equestrian, and Musical Fund, at Willis's Rooms, and in proposing the toast of the evening, said :

"I rest the strong claim of the society for its useful existence and its truly charitable functions on a very few words, though, as well as I can recollect, upon something like six grounds. First, it relieves the sick; secondly, it buries the dead; thirdly, it enables the poor members of the profession to journey to accept new engagements whenever they find themselves stranded in some remote, inhospitable place, or when, from other circumstances, they find themselves perfectly crippled as to locomotion for want of money; fourthly, it often finds such engagements for them by acting as their honest, disinterested agent; fifthly, it is its principle to act humanely upon the instant, and never, as is too often the case within my experience, to beat about the bush till the bush is withered and dead; lastly, the society is not in the least degree exclusive, but takes under its compre hensive care the whole range of the theatre and the concert-room, from the manager in his room of state, or in his caravan, or at the drum-head—down to the theatrical housekeeper, who is usually to be found among the cobwebs and the flies, or down to the hall-porter, who passes his life in a thorough draught—and, to the best of my observation, in perpetually interrupted endeavours to eat something with a knife and fork out of a basin, by a dusty fire, in that extraordinary little gritty room, upon which the sun never shines, and on the portals of which are inscribed the magic words ' stage-door.' "

. . . . . . "Struggling artists must necessarily change from place to place, and thus it frequently happens that they become, as it were, strangers in every place, and very slight circumstances—a passing illness, the sickness of the husband, wife, or child, a serious town, an anathematising expounder of the gospel of gentleness and forbearance—any one of these causes may often in a few hours wreck them upon a rock in the barren ocean; and then, happily, this society, with the swift alacrity of the life-boat, dashes to the rescue, and takes them off." . . . . . . "There is no class of society the members of which so well help themselves, or so well help each other. Not in the whole grand chapters of Westminster Abbey and York Minster, not in the whole quadrangle of the Royal Exchange, not in the whole list of members of the Stock Exchange, not in the Inns of Court, not in the College of Physicians, not in the College of Surgeons, can there possibly be found more remarkable instances of uncomplaining poverty, of cheerful, constant self-denial, of the generous remembrance of the claims of kindred and professional brotherhood, than will certainly be found in the dingiest and dirtiest concert-room, in the least lucid theatre—even in the raggedest tent circus that was ever stained by weather. I have been twitted in print before now with rather flattering actors when I address them as one of their trustees at their General Fund dinner. Believe me, I flatter nobody, unless it be sometimes myself; but in such a company as the present I always feel it my manful duty to bear my testimony to this fact—first, because it is opposed to a stupid, unfeeling libel; secondly, because my doing so may afford some slight encouragement to the persons who are unjustly depreciated; and lastly, and most of all, because I know it is the truth."

In proposing the toast of "The Ladies" on this occasion Dickens made happy and appreciative allusion to one who is still one of the most deservedly popular actresses on our stage:—"It is the privilege of this society annually to hear a lady speak for her own sex. Who so competent to do this as Mrs. Stirling? Surely one who has so gracefully and so captivatingly, with such an exquisite mixture of art, and fancy, and fidelity, represented her own sex in innumerable characters, under an infinite variety of phases, cannot fail to represent them well in her own character, especially when it is, amidst her many triumphs, the most agreeable of all. I beg to propose to you 'The Ladies,' and I will couple with that toast the name of Mrs. Stirling."

On April 6th, 1846, Dickens took the chair at the first anniversary festival of the General Theatrical Fund Association, and in the course of the speech in which he proposed the toast of the evening said :

"Let us ever remember that there is no class of actors who stand so much in need of a retiring fund as those who do not win the great prizes, but who are nevertheless an essential part of the theatrical system, and by consequence bear a part in contributing to our pleasures. We owe them a debt which we ought to pay. The beds of such men are not of roses, but of very artificial flowers indeed. Their lives are lives of care and privation, and hard struggles with very stern realities. It is among the poor actors who drink wine from goblets, in colour marvellously like toast-and-water, and who preside at Parmecide feasts with wonderful appetites for steaks,—it is from their ranks that the most triumphant favourites have sprung. And surely, besides this, the greater the instruction and delight we derive from the rich English drama, the more we are bound to succour and protect the humblest of those votaries of the art who add to our instruction and amusement.

"Hazlitt has well said that 'There is no class of society whom so many persons regard with affection as actors. We greet them on the stage, we like to meet them in the streets; they always recall to us pleasant associations.' When they have strutted and fretted their hour upon the stage, let them not be heard no more—but let them be heard sometimes to say that they are happy in their old age. When they have passed for the last time from behind that glittering row of lights with which we are all familiar, let them not pass away into gloom and darkness—but let them pass into cheerfulness and light—into a contented and happy home.

"This is the object for which we have met; and I am too familiar with the English character not to know that it will be effected. When we come suddenly in a crowded street upon the careworn features of a familiar face—crossing us like the ghost of pleasant hours long forgotten—let us not recall those features with pain, in sad remembrance of what they once were, but let us in joy recognise it, and go back a pace or two to meet it once again, as that of a friend who has beguiled us of a moment of care, who has taught us to sympathise with virtuous grief, cheating us to tears for sorrows not our own—and we all know how pleasant are such tears. Let such a face be ever remembered as that of our benefactor and our friend.

"I tried to recollect, in coming here, whether I had ever been in any theatre in my life from which I had not brought away some pleasant association, however poor the theatre, and I protest, out of my varied experience, I could not remember even one from which I had not brought some favourable impression, and that, commencing with the period when I believed the clown was a being born into the world with infinite pockets, and ending with that in which I saw the other night, outside one of the 'Royal Saloons,' a playbill which showed me ships completely rigged, carrying men, and careering over boundless and tempestuous oceans. And now, bespeaking your kindest remembrance of our theatres and actors, I beg to propose that you drink as heartily and freely as ever a toast was drunk in this toast-drinking city, 'Prosperity to the General Theatrical Fund.'"

On April 14th, 1851, the sixth annual dinner of the General Fund was held at the London Tavern. Dickens occupied the chair, and in the course of his speech said :

"This is a theatrical association, expressly adapted to the wants and to the means of the whole theatrical profession all over England. It is a society in which the word exclusiveness is wholly unknown. It is a society which includes every actor, whether he be Benedict, or Hamlet, or the Ghost, or the Bandit, or the Court Physician, or, in the one person, the whole King's army. He may do the 'light business,' or the 'heavy,' or the comic, or the eccentric. He may be the captain who courts the young lady, whose uncle still unaccountably persists in dressing himself in a costume one hundred years older than his time. Or he may be the young lady's brother in the white gloves and inexpressibles, whose duty in the family appears to be to listen to the female members of it whenever they sing, and to shake hands with everybody between all the verses. Or he be may the baron who gives the *fête*, and who sits uneasily on the sofa under a canopy with the baroness while the *fête* is going on. Or he may be the peasant at the *fête* who comes on the stage to swell the drinking chorus, and who, it may be observed, always turns his glass upside down before he begins to drink out of it. Or he may be the clown who takes away the doorstep of the house where the evening party is going on. Or he may be the gentleman who issues out of the house on the false alarm, and is precipitated into the area. Or, to come to the actresses, she may be the fairy who resides for ever in a revolving star with an occasional visit to a bower or a palace. Or the actor may be the armed head of the witch's cauldron; or even that extraordinary witch, concerning whom I have observed in country places, that he is much less like the notion formed from the description of Hopkins than the Malcolm or Donalbain of the previous scenes. The society, in short, says, 'Be you what you may, be you actor or actress, be your path in the profession never so high, or never so low, never so haughty, or never so humble, we offer you the means of doing good to yourselves, and of doing good to your brethren.'"

. . . . . . "I have used the word gratitude; and let any man ask his own heart, and confess if we have not some grateful acknowledgments for the actors' art? Not peculiarly because it is a profession often pursued, and as it were marked, by poverty and misfortune,—for other callings, God knows, have their distresses—nor because the actor has sometimes to come from scenes of sickness, of suffering, ay, even of death itself, to play his part before us—for all of us, in our spheres, have as often to do violence to our feelings and to hide our hearts in fighting this great battle of life and in discharging our duties and responsibilities. But the art of the actor excites reflections, sombre or grotesque, awful or humorous, which we are all familiar with. If any man were to tell me that he denied his acknowledgments to the stage, I would simply put to him one question—'Whether he remembered his first play?'

"If you, gentlemen, will but carry back your recollection to that great night, and call to mind the bright and harmless world which then opened to your view, we shall, I think, hear favourably of the effect upon your liberality on this occasion from our secretary."

On the evening of March 1st, 1851, the friends and admirers of Mr. Macready entertained him at a public dinner. Sir E. B. Lytton took the chair, and in proposing his health, and alluding to Macready's farewell benefit at Drury Lane, on which occasion he played the part of Macbeth, Dickens said:

"When I looked round on the vast assemblage, and observed the huge pit hushed into stillness on the rising of the curtain, and that mighty surging gallery, where men in their shirt-sleeves had been striking out their arms like strong swimmers—when I saw that boisterous human flood become still water in a moment, and remain so from the opening to the end of the play, it suggested to me something besides the trustworthiness of an English crowd, and the delusion under which those labour who are apt to disparage and malign it; it suggested to me that in meeting here to-night we undertook to represent something of the all-pervading feeling of that crowd, through all its intermediate degrees, from the full-dressed lady, with her diamonds sparkling in her breast in the proscenium box, to the half-undressed gentleman who bides his time to take some refreshment in the back row of the gallery."

CHAPTER VII.

THE STAGE IN HIS LETTERS.

SCATTERED about among these pages are passages from the delightful letters of Charles Dickens bearing upon theatrical subjects, and in this chapter it is proposed to give further extracts from that happily preserved treasure-house. This will most conveniently be done by merely quoting them in their proper chronological order.

1836. *(To Mr. John Hullah, concerning " The Village Coquettes.")*

" Have you seen *The Examiner?* It is rather depreciatory of the opera; but, like all inveterate critiques against Braham, so well done that I cannot help laughing at it, for the life and soul of me. I have seen *The Sunday Times, The Dispatch,* and *The Satirist,* all of which blow their critic trumpets against unhappy me most lustily. Either I must have grievously awakened the ire of all the ' adaptors ' and their friends, or the drama must be decidedly bad. I haven't made up my mind yet which of the two is the fact."

1837. *(To Mr. J. P. Harley.)*

"I have considered the terms on which I could afford just now to sell Mr. Braham the acting copyright in London of an entirely new piece for the St. James's Theatre; and I could not sit down to write one in a single act of about one hour long, under a hundred pounds. For a new piece in two acts, a hundred and fifty pounds would be the sum I should require.

"I do not know whether, with reference to arrangements that were made with any other writers, this may, or may not, appear a large item. I state it merely with regard to the value of my own time and writings at this moment. . . ."

1838. *(To Mr. W. C. Macready, concerning "The Lamplighter.")*

"I have not seen you for the past week, because I hoped when we next met to bring 'The Lamplighter' in my hand. . . . I am afraid to name any particular day, but I pledge myself that you shall have it this month, and you may calculate on that promise. I send you with this a copy of a farce I wrote for Harley when he left Drury Lane, and in which he acted for some seventy nights. It is the best thing he does. It is barely possible you might like to try it. Any local or temporary allusions could be easily altered. . . . P.S. For Heaven's sake don't fancy that I hold 'The Strange Gentleman' in any estimation, or have a wish upon the subject."

December 13th, 1838. (*The Same.*)
"I can have but one opinion on the subject—withdraw the farce at once, by all means. . . . Believe me that I have no other feeling of disappointment connected with this matter but that arising from the not having been able to be of some use to you."

May 21st, 1842. (*To Professor Felton, concerning Amateur Theatricals at Montreal.*)
"I would give something . . . . if you could stumble into that very dark and dusty theatre in the day-time (at any minute between twelve and three), and see me with my coat off, the stage manager and universal director, urging impracticable ladies and impossible gentlemen on to the very confines of insanity, shouting and driving about, in my own person, to an extent which would justify any philanthropic stranger in clapping me into a strait-waistcoat without further inquiry, endeavouring to goad H. into some dim and faint understanding of a prompter's duties, and struggling in such a vortex of noise, dirt, bustle, confusion, and inextricable entangle-

ment of speech and action as you would grow giddy in contemplating. . . . This kind of voluntary hard labour used to be my great delight. The *furor* has come upon me again, and I begin to be once more of opinion that nature intended me for the lessee of a national theatre, and that pen, ink, and paper have spoiled a manager."

November 12th, 1842. *(To Mr. W. C. Macready, concerning " The Patrician's Daughter.")*

"The more I think of Marston's play, the more sure I feel that a prologue to the purpose would help it materially, and almost decide the fate of any ticklish point on the first night. Now I have an idea . . . . that would take the prologue out of the conventional dress of prologues, quite. Get the curtain up with a dash, and begin the play with a sledge-hammer blow. If, on consideration, you should think with me, I will write the prologue heartily."

(The Same.)

" One suggestion, though it be a late one. Do have upon the table, in the opening scene of the second act, something in a velvet case, or frame, that may look like a large miniature of Mabel, such as one of Ross's, and eschew that picture.

It haunts me with a sense of danger. Even a titter, at that critical time, with the whole of that act before you, would be a fatal thing. The picture is bad in itself, bad in its effect upon the beautiful room, bad in all its associations with the house."

September 1st, 1843. *(To Professor Felton, concerning Macready.)*

"He is one of the noblest fellows in the world, and I would give a great deal that you and I should sit beside each other to see him play Virginius, Lear, or Werner, which I take to be, every way, the greatest piece of exquisite perfection that his lofty art is capable of attaining. His Macbeth, especially the last act, is a tremendous reality; but so, indeed, is almost everything he does."

January 2nd, 1844. *(The Same.)*
"Of course you like Macready. . . . . I wish you could see him play Lear. It is stupendously terrible."

November 13th, 1843. *(To Mr. R. H. Horne, concerning "The Village Coquettes," &c.)*
"Pray tell that besotted —— to let the opera sink into its native obscurity. I did it in a fit of d——ble good nature long ago, for Hullah,

who wrote some very pretty music to it. I just put down for everybody what everybody at the St. James's Theatre wanted to say and do, and that they could say and do best, and I have been most sincerely repentant ever since. The farce I also did as a sort of practical joke, for Harley,* whom I had known a long time. It was funny— adapted from one of the published sketches called the 'Great Winglebury Duel,' and was published by Chapman and Hall. But I have no copy of it now, nor should I think they have. But both these things were done without the least consideration or regard to reputation.

"I wouldn't repeat them for a thousand pounds apiece, and devoutly wish them to be forgotten."

1844. (*To Mr. Forster, concerning a representation in Italy of Dumas's " Kean."*

"There was a mysterious person called the Prince of Var-lees (Wales), the youngest and slimmest man in the company, whose badinage in Kean's dressing-room was irresistible; and the dresser wore top-boots, a Greek skull cap, a black velvet jacket, and leather breeches. One or two of the actors looked very hard at me to see how I was touched by these English pecu-

---

* *i.e.* "The Strange Gentleman."

liarities, especially when Kean kissed his male friends on both cheeks."

1844. (*To Mr. Robert Keeley concerning an adaptation of "Martin Chuzzlewit."*)

" I cannot consistently, with the opinion I hold, and have always held, in reference to the principle of adapting novels for the stage, give you a prologue to 'Chuzzlewit.' But believe me to be quite sincere in saying that if I felt I could reasonably do such a thing for anyone, I would do it for you. . . . . I presume Mrs. Keeley will do Ruth Pinch. If so, I feel secure about her, and of Mrs. Gamp I am certain. But a queer sensation begins in my legs, and comes upwards to my forehead, when I think of Tom."

August 24th, 1844. (*To Mr. Clarkson Stanfield.*)

"We have had weather here, since five o'clock this morning, after your own heart. Suppose yourself the Admiral in 'Black-Eyed Susan,' after the acquittal of William, and when it was possible to be on friendly terms with him. I am T. P. (T. P. Cooke). My trousers are very full at the ankles, my black neckerchief is tied in the regular style, the name of my ship is painted round my glazed hat, I have a red waistcoat on, and the seams of my blue jacket are 'paid'—permit me to dig you in the ribs when I make use of this nautical expression—in white. In my hand I hold the very box connected with the story of Sandomingerbilly. I lift up my eyebrows as far as I can (on the T. P. model), take a quid from the box, screw the lid on again (chewing at the same time and looking pleasantly at the pit), brush it with my right elbow, take up my right leg, scrape my right foot on the ground, hitch up my trousers, and in reply to a question of yours, namely, ' Indeed, what weather, William?' I deliver myself as follows:

" ' Lord love your honour! Weather! Such weather as would set all hands to the pumps aboard one of your fresh-water cockboats, and set the purser to his wits' end to stow away, for the use of the ship's company, the casks full of blue water as would come powering in over the gunnel! The dirtiest night, your honour, as ever you see 'atween Spithead at gun-fire and the Bay of Biscay! The wind sou'-west, and your house dead in the wind's eye; the breakers running up high upon the rocky beads, the light'us no more looking thro' the fog than Davy Jones's sarser eye through the blue sky of heaven in a calm, or the blue top-lights of your honour's lady cast down in a modest overhauling of her cat-heads; avast (*whistling*) my dear eyes, here am I a-goin' ahead on to the breakers.' (*bowing*).

"*Admiral (smiling).* 'No, William! I admire plain speaking, as you know, and so does old England, William, and old England's Queen. But you were saying——'

"*William.* 'Aye, aye, your honour (*scratching his head*), I've lost my reckoning. Damme!—I ast pardon—but won't your honour throw a hencoop on any old end of towline to a man as is overboard?'

"*Admiral (smiling still).* 'You were saying, William, that the wind——'

"*William (again cocking his leg and slapping the thighs very hard).* 'Avast heaving, your honour. . . . . .*

"*Admiral.* 'You have described it well, William, and I thank you. But who are these?'

"*Enter Supers in calico jackets to look like cloth, some in brown holland petticoat-trousers and big boots, all with very large buckles. Last Super rolls in a cask, and pretends to keep it. Other Supers apply their mugs to the bunghole, and drink, previously holding them upside down.*

---

* NOTE.—There is no occasion to quote "William's" next speech in full. The object of the extract is to show the marvellous power that (had he chosen to exercise it) Dickens possessed as a writer of stage travesty. Another delicious specimen of this style of writing is to be found in a letter dated January 16th, 1854, and addressed to Miss Mary Boyle, in which an imaginary Falkland and Acres scene in "The Rivals" is admirably burlesqued.

"*William (after shaking hands with everybody).* '. Who are these, your Honour? Messmates as staunch and true as ever broke biscuit. Ain't you, my lads?'

"*All.* 'Aye, aye, William. That we are! that we are!'

"*Admiral (much affected).* 'Oh, England! what wonder that——! But I will no longer detain you from your sports, my humble friends'—(*Admiral speaks very low, and looks hard at the orchestra, this being the cue for the dance*)— 'from your sports, my humble friends. Farewell!'

'*All.* 'Hurrah! hurrah!' (*exit Admiral.*)

,'*Voice behind.* 'Suppose the dance, Mr. Stanfield. Are you all ready? Go, then!'"

September 15th, 1845.—(*To Mr. W. C. Macready.*)

" N.B. Observe.—I think of changing my present mode of life, and am open to an engagement.

"N.B. No. 2.—I will undertake not to play tragedy, though passion is my strength."

November 27th, 1846.—(*To M. de Cerjat.*)

"Keeley and his wife are making great preparations for producing the Christmas story" ("The Battle of Life,") "and I have made them (as an old stage manager) carry out one or two expensive notions of mine about scenery and so forth—in particular a sudden change from the inside of the doctor's house, in the midst of the ball, to the orchard in the snow—which ought to tell very well. But actors are so bad, in general, and the best are spread over so many theatres, that the 'cast' is black despair and moody madness."

December 19th, 1846.—(*To Mrs. Charles Dickens.*)

"I really am bothered to death by this confounded *dramatisation* of the Christmas book . . . I must exempt, however, from the general slackness, both the Keeleys. I hope they will be very good. I have never seen anything of its kind better than the manner in which they played the little supper scene between Clemency and Britain yesterday. It was quite perfect, even to me."

January 28th, 1847.—*Concerning the French stage.)*

"'Clarissa Harlowe' is still the rage. There are some things in it rather calculated to astonish the ghost of Richardson, but Clarissa is very admirably played" (by Rose Chéri), "and dies better than the original, to my thinking; but

Richardson is no great favourite of mine, and never seems to me to take his top-boots off, whatever he does. Several pieces are in course of representation, involving rare portraits of the English. In one, a servant, called 'Tom Bob,' who wears a particularly English waistcoat, trimmed with gold lace and concealing his ankles, does very good things indeed. In another, a Prime Minister of England, who has ruined himself by railway speculations, hits off some of our national characteristics very happily, frequently making incidental mention of 'Vishmingster,' 'Regeen Street,' and other places with which you are well acquainted. 'Sir Fakson' is one of the characters in another play—'English to the Core'; and I saw a Lord Mayor of London at one of the small theatres the other night, looking uncommonly well in a stage-coachman's waistcoat, the Order of the Garter, and a very low-crowned, broad-brimmed hat, not unlike a dustman."

February 14th, 1847 :—

"Shall I ever forget Vestris,* in 'London

---

* NOTE.—Those who are versed in theatrical lore will remember that Madame Vestris and Harley were the original Grace Harkaway and Mark Meddle in Boucicault's well-known comedy, originally produced at Covent Garden Theatre in 1841,—and playgoers of to-day may recognise the fact that the same artificial, but theatrically-effective lines, make the same impression upon an ordinary audience now as they did nearly fifty years ago.

Assurance,' bursting out with certain praises (they always elicited three rounds) of a—of a country morning, I think it was. The atrocity was perpetrated, I remember, on a lawn before a villa. It was led up to by flower-pots. The thing was as like any honest sympathy, or honest English, as the rose-pink on a sweep's face on May-day is to a beautiful complexion; but Harley generally appeared touched to the soul, and a man in the pit always cried out, 'Beau-ti-ful!'"

November 7th, 1848.—(*To Mr. Effingham William Wilson, concerning "A National Theatre."*)

"That such a theatre as you describe would be but worthy of this nation, and would not stand low upon the list of its instructors, I have no kind of doubt. I wish I could cherish a stronger faith than I have in the probability of its establishment on a rational footing within fifty years."

1849.—(*To Mr. Forster.*)

"Poor Regnier has lost his only child. . . . Poole was at the funeral, and writes that he never saw, or could have imagined, such intensity of grief as Regnier's at the grave. How one loves him for it. But is it not always true, in comedy and in tragedy, that the more real the man, the more genuine the actor?"

January 5th, 1851.—(*To Sir Edward Bulwer Lytton, concerning "Not So Bad As We Seem."*)

"I think it *most admirable*. Full of character, strong in interest, rich in capital situations, and *certain to go nobly*. You know how highly I thought of 'Money,' but I sincerely think these three acts finer. . . . I cannot say too much of the comedy to express what I think and feel concerning it; and I look at it, too, remember, with the yellow eye of an actor! I should have taken to it (need I say so!) *con amore* in any case, but I should have been jealous of your reputation, exactly as I appreciate your generosity. If I had a misgiving of ten lines I should have scrupulously mentioned it. . . . This brings me to my own part. If we had anyone, or could get anyone, for Wilmot, I could do (I think) something so near your meaning in Sir Gilbert, that I let him go with a pang. Assumption has charms for me—I hardly know for how many wild reasons—so delightful, that I feel a loss of, oh! I can't say what exquisite foolery, when I lose a chance of being some one in voice, etc., not at all like myself. But—I speak quite freely, knowing you will not mistake me—I know from experience that we could find nobody to hold the play together in Wilmot if I didn't do it. I think I could touch the gallant, generous, careless pretence, with the real man at the bottom of it, so as to take the audience with him from the first scene. . . . . P.S.—I have forgotten something. I suggest this title: 'Knowing the World; or, Not So Bad as We Seem.'"

May 9th, 1853.—(*To Mons. Regnier.*)
"There is a certain Miss Kelly, now sixty-two years old, who was once one of the very best of English actresses, in the greater and better days of the English theatre. She has much need of a benefit, and I am exerting myself to arrange one for her, on about the 9th June, if possible, at the St. James's Theatre. . . . . It would be a great attraction to the public, and a great proof of friendship to me, if you would act."

May 20th, 1853.—(*To the Same.*)
"I am heartily obliged to you for your kind letter respecting Miss Kelly's benefit. . . . . Mitchell, like a brave *garçon* as he is, most willingly consents to your acting for us."

Boulogne, August 24th, 1853.—(*To Mr. W. C. Macready.*)
"I saw 'The Midsummer Night's Dream' at

the Opéra Comique, done here (very well) last night. The way in which a poet named Willyim Shay Kes Peer gets drunk in company with Sir John Foll Stayffe, fights with a noble 'night, Lor Latimeer (who is in love with a maid-of-honour you may have read of in history, called Mees Oleevia), and promises not to do so any more on observing symptoms of love for him in the Queen of England, is very remarkable. Queen Elizabeth, too, in the profound and impenetrable disguise of a black velvet mask, two inches deep by three broad, following him into taverns and worse places, and enquiring of persons of doubtful reputation for 'the sublime Williams,' was inexpressibly ridiculous. And yet the nonsense was done with a sense quite admirable."

Paris, February 16th, 1855. — (*To Miss Hogarth.*)

"'La Joie fait Peur' at the Français delighted me. Exquisitely played and beautifully imagined altogether. Last night we went to the Porte St. Martin to see a piece (English subject) called 'Jane Osborne,' which the characters pronounce 'Ja Nosbornne.' The seducer was Lord Nottingham. The comic Englishwoman's name (she kept lodgings and was a very bad character) was Missees Christmas. She had begun to get into great difficulties with a gentleman of the name of Meestair Cornhill, when we were obliged to leave, at the end of the first act, by the intolerable stench of the place."

Paris, 1855-56.—(*To Mr. Forster.*)
"Incomparably the finest acting I ever saw, I saw last night at the Ambigu. They have revived that old piece, once immensely popular in London under the name of 'Thirty Years of a Gambler's Life.' Old Lemaitre plays his famous character, and never did I see anything, in art, so exaltedly horrible and awful. In the earlier acts he was so well made up, and so light and active, that he really looked sufficiently young. But in the last two, when he had grown old and miserable, he did the finest things I really believe, that are within the power of acting. Two or three times, a great cry of horror went all round the house. When he met, in the inn yard, the traveller whom he murders, and first saw his money, the manner in which the crime came into his head—and eyes—was as truthful as it was terrific. This traveller, being a good fellow, gives him wine. You should see the dim remembrance of his better days that comes over him as he takes the glass, and, in a strange dazed way, makes as if he were going to touch the other man's, or do some airy thing

with it, and then stops and flings the contents down his hot throat, as if he were pouring it into a lime-kiln. But this was nothing to what follows after he has done the murder, and comes home, with a basket of provisions, a ragged pocket full of money, and a badly washed bloody right hand—which his little girl finds out. After the child asked him if he had hurt his hand, his going aside, turning himself round, and looking over all his clothes for spots, was so inexpressibly dreadful that it really scared one. He called for wine, and the sickness that came upon him when he saw the colour, was one of the things that brought out the curious cry I have spoken of, from the audience. Then he fell into a sort of bloody mist, and went on to the end groping about with no mind for anything, except making his fortune by staking this money, and a faint, dull kind of love for the child. . . . And such a dress; such a face; and, above all, such an extraordinary guilty, wicked thing as he made of a knotted branch of a tree which was his walking-stick, from the moment when the idea of the murder came into his head! . . . . He got half-boastful of that walking-staff to himself, and half afraid of it; and didn't know whether to be grimly pleased that it had the jagged end or to hate it, and be horrified at it. He sat at a little table in the inn-yard, drinking with the traveller; and this horrible stick got between them like the Devil, while he counted on his fingers the uses he could put the money to."

"In 'Comme il vous Plaira' (a French version of 'As You Like It,') nobody had anything to do but to sit down as often as possible on as many stones and trunks of trees as possible. When I had seen Jacques seat himself on 17 roots of trees, and 25 grey stones, which was at the end of the second act, I came away."

"Scribe and his wife were of the party, but had to go away at the ice-time because it was the first representation at the Opéra Comique of a new opera by Auber and himself, of which very great expectations have been formed. It was very curious to see him—the author of 400 pieces—getting nervous as the time approached, and pulling out his watch every minute. At last he dashed out as if he were going into what a friend of mine calls a plunge bath."

"By-the-bye, I see a fine actor lost in Scribe. In all his pieces he has everything done in his own way; and on that same night he was showing what Rachel did not do, and wouldn't do, in the last scene of 'Adrienne Lecouvreur,' with extraordinary force and intensity."

Paris, January 19th, 1856.—(*To Mr. Wilkie Collins*).

"At the Porte St. Martin they are doing the 'Orestes,' put into French verse by Alexandre Dumas. Really one of the absurdest things I ever saw. The scene of the tomb, with all manner of classical females, in black, grouping themselves on the lid, and on the steps, and on each other, and in every conceivable aspect of obtrusive impossibility, is just like the window of one of those artists in hair, who address the friends of deceased persons."

January 9th, 1857.—(*To Sir James Emmerson Tennent, concerning private theatricals*).

"As to the play itself; when it is made as good as my care can make it, I derive a strange feeling out of it, like writing a book in company; a satisfaction of a most singular kind, which has no exact parallel in my life; a something that I suppose to belong to the life of a labourer in art alone, and which has to me a conviction of its being actual truth without its pain, that I never could adequately state if I were to try never so hard. . . . I assure you it has been a remarkable lesson to my young people in patience, perseverance, punctuality, and order; and, best of all, in that kind of humility which is got from the earned knowledge that whatever the right hand finds to do must be done with the heart in it, and in a desperate earnest."

—1857, Doncaster (*To Mr. Forster, concerning a performance of Lord Lytton's "Money."*)

"I have rarely seen anything finer than Lord Glossmore, a chorus-singer in bluchers, drab trousers, and a brown sack; and Dudley Smooth, in somebody else's wig, hindside before. Stout also, in anything he could lay hold of. The waiter at the club had an immense moustache, white trousers, and a striped jacket; and he brought everybody who came in a vinegar cruet. The man who read the will began thus: 'I so-and-so, being of unsound mind but firm of body.' In spite of all this, however, the real character, humour, wit, and good writing of the comedy, made themselves apparent; and the applause was loud and repeated, and really seemed genuine. Its capital things were not lost altogether. It was succeeded by a jockey dance by five ladies, who put their whips in their mouths and worked imaginary winners up to the float—an immense success."

December 28th, 1860. (*To Miss Mary Boyle.*)
"On Boxing Night I was at Covent Garden. A dull pantomime was 'worked' (as we say) better than I ever saw a heavy piece worked on a first

night, until suddenly and without a moment's warning, every scene on that immense stage fell over on its face, and disclosed chaos by gaslight behind! There never was such a business; about sixty people who were on the stage being extinguished in the most remarkable manner. Not a soul was hurt. In the uproar some moon-calf rescued a porter pot six feet high (out of which the clown had been drinking when the accident happened), and stood it on the cushion of the lowest proscenium box, P.S., beside a lady and gentleman, who were dreadfully ashamed of it. The moment the house knew that nobody was injured, they directed their whole attention to this gigantic porter pot in its genteel position (the lady and gentleman trying to hide behind it), and roared with laughter. When a modest footman came from behind the curtain to clear it, and took it up in his arms like a Brobdingnagian baby, we all laughed more than ever we had laughed in our lives. I don't know why."

January 24th, 1862. (*To Sir Edward Bulwer Lytton, concerning a proposed operatic version of " The Lady of Lyons."*)

"I do *not* think the production of such an opera in the slightest degree likely to injure the play or render it a less valuable property than it is now. If it could have any effect upon so standard and popular a work as 'The Lady of Lyons,' the effect would, in my judgment, be beneficial. But I believe the play to be high above any such influence. Assuming you do consent to the adaptation, in a desire to oblige Oxenford, I would not recommend your asking any pecuniary compensation. This for two reasons: firstly, because the compensation could only be small at the best; secondly, because your taking it would associate you (unreasonably, but not the less assuredly) with the opera. The only objection I descry is purely one of feeling. Pauline trotting about in front of the float, invoking the orchestra with a limp pocket-handkerchief, is a notion that makes goose-flesh of my back. Also a yelping tenor going away to the wars in a scena half-an-hour long is painful to contemplate. Damas, too, as a bass, with a grizzled bald head, blatantly bellowing about:

> "Years long ago
> When the sound of the drum
> First made his blood glow
> With a rum ti tum tum,"

rather sticks in my throat; but there really seems to me to be no other objection, if you can get over this."

December 6th, 1862. (*To Mons. Charles Fechter.*)

"I have read 'The White Rose' attentively,

and think it an extremely good play. It is vigorously written with a great knowledge of the stage, and presents many striking situations. I think the close particularly fine, impressive, bold, and new. But I greatly doubt the expediency of your doing *any* historical play early in your management. By the words 'historical play,' I mean a play founded on any incident in English history. Our public are accustomed to associate historical plays with Shakespeare. In any other hands, I believe they care very little for crowns and dukedoms. What you want is something with an interest of a more domestic and general nature—an interest as romantic as you please, but having a more general and wider response than a disputed succession to the throne can have for Englishmen at this time of day. Such interest culminated in the last Stuart, and has worn itself out. It would be uphill work to evoke an interest in Perkin Warbeck.

"I do not doubt the play's being well received, but my fear is that these people would be looked upon as mere abstractions, and would have but a cold welcome in consequence, and would not lay hold of your audience. Now when you *have* laid hold of your audience and have accustomed them to your theatre, you may produce 'The White Rose,' with far greater justice to the author, and to the manager also. Wait. Feel your way. Perkin Warbeck is too far removed from analogy with the sympathies and lives of the people for a beginning."

February 19th, 1863.—(*To Mr. W. C. Macready.*)

"Paris generally is about as wicked and extravagant as in the days of the Regency. Madame Viardot in the 'Orphée,' most splendid. An opera of 'Faust,' a very sad and noble rendering of that sad and noble story. Stage management remarkable for some admirable, and really poetical, effects of light. In the more striking situations, Mephistopheles surrounded by an infernal red atmosphere of his own. Marguerite by a pale blue mournful light. The two never blending. After Marguerite has taken the jewels placed in her way in the garden, a weird evening draws on, and the bloom fades from the flowers, and the leaves of the trees droop and lose their fresh green, and mournful shadows overhang her chamber window, which was innocently bright and gay at first. I couldn't bear it, and gave in completely.

"Fechter doing wonders over the way here,* with a picturesque French drama. Miss Kate Terry, in a small part in it, perfectly charming.

* The letter is dated from the office of "All the Year Round."

You may remember her making a noise, years ago, doing a boy in an inn, in 'The Courier of Lyons'? She has a tender love-scene in this piece, which is a really beautiful and artistic thing. I saw her do it at about three in the morning of the day when the theatre opened, surrounded by shavings and carpenters, and (of course) with that inevitable hammer going; and I told Fechter: 'That is the very best piece of womanly tenderness I have ever seen on the stage, and you'll find that no audience can miss it.' It is a comfort to add that it was instantly seized upon, and is much talked of."

1864 (?).—(*To Mr. John Forster.*)

"I have been cautioning Fechter about the play whereof he gave the plot and scenes to B; and out of which I have struck some enormities, my account of which will (I think) amuse you. It has one of the best first acts I ever saw; but if he can do much with the last two, not to say three, there are resources in his art that *I* know nothing about. When I went over the play this day week, he was at least twenty minutes, *in a boat, in the last scene*, discussing with another gentleman (also in the boat) whether he should kill him or not; after which the gentleman dived over and swam for it. Also, in the most important and dangerous parts of the play, there was a young person of the name of Pickles who was constantly being mentioned by name, in conjunction with the powers of light or darkness; as, 'Great Heaven! Pickles?' 'By Hell, 'tis Pickles!' 'Pickles? a thousand Devils!'—— 'Distraction! Pickles?'"

1864.—(*To Mr. John Forster.*)

"I went the other night to see 'The Streets of London' at the Princess's. A piece that is really drawing all the town, and filling the house with nightly overflows. It is the most depressing instance, without exception, of an utterly degraded and debased theatrical taste that has ever come under my writhing notice. For not only do the audiences—of all classes—go, but they are unquestionably delighted. At Astley's there has been much puffing at great cost of a certain Miss Ada Isaacs Menken, who is to be seen bound on the horse in 'Mazeppa' 'ascending the fearful precipices, not as hitherto done by a dummy.' Last night, having a boiling head, I went out from here to cool myself on Waterloo Bridge, and I thought I would go and see this heroine. . . . . Now who do you think the lady is? If you do not already know, ask that question of the highest Irish mountains that look eternal, and they'll never tell you—*Mrs. Heenan!* Contrariwise I assisted the other night at the Adelphi and saw quite an admirable performance of Mr. Toole and Mrs. Mellon—she, an old servant, wonderfully like Anne—he, showing a power of passion very unusual indeed in a comic actor, as such things go, and of a quite remarkable kind."

September 16th, 1867.—(*To Mons. Charles Fechter concerning* "*The Lady of Lyons.*")

"Going over the prompt-book carefully, I see one change in your part to which (on Lytton's behalf) I positively object, as I am quite certain he would not consent to it. It is highly injudicious besides, as striking out the best known line in the play. Turn to your part in Act III., the speech beginning:

> 'Pauline, *by pride*
> *Angels have fallen ere thy time:* by pride:'

"You have made a passage farther on stand

> '*Then did I seek to rise*
> *Out of my mean estate. Thy bright image,*' etc.

"I must stipulate for your restoring it thus:

> 'Then did I seek to rise
> Out of the prison of my mean estate;
> And with such jewels as the exploring mind
> Brings from the caves of Knowledge, buy my ransom
> From those twin jailers of the daring heart—
> Low birth and iron fortune. Thy bright image,' etc., etc.

The last figure has been again and again quoted;

it is identified with the play; it is fine in itself; and above all, I KNOW that Lytton would not let it go. In writing to him to-day, fully explaining the changes in detail, and saying that I disapprove of nothing else, I have told him that I notice this change, and that I immediately let you know that it must not be made.

"(There will not be a man in the house from any newspaper who would not detect mutilations in that speech, moreover.)"

October 25th, 1867. (*To Lord Lytton, concerning his play, " The Captives."*)

"I have read the play with great attention, interest, and admiration; and I need not say to *you*, that the art of it—the fine construction—the exquisite nicety of the touches—with which it is brought out, have been a study to me, in the pursuit of which I have had extraordinary relish. . . . Now, as to the classical ground and manners of the play. I suppose the objection to the Greek dress to be already—as De Foe would write it—'gotten over' by your suggestion. I suppose the dress not to be conventionally associated with stilts and boredom, but to be new to the public eye and very picturesque. Grant all that;—the names remain. Now not only used such names to be inseparable in the public mind from stately weariness, but of late days they have become inseparable in the same public mind from silly puns upon the names, and from burlesque. You do no not know (I hope, at least, for my friend's sake) what the Strand Theatre is. A Greek name, and a break-down nigger dance, have become inseparable there. I do not mean to say that your genius may not be too powerful for such associations; but I do most positively mean to say that you would lose half the play in overcoming them. At the best, you would have to contend against them during the first three acts. The old tendency to become frozen on classical ground would be in the best part of the audience; the new tendency to titter on such ground would be in the worst part. And instead of starting fair with the audience, it is my conviction that you would start with them against you, and would have to win them over."

May 22nd, 1868. (*To Mons. Fechter, concerning* "*No Thoroughfare.*")

"I have an idea about the bedroom act, which I should certainly have suggested if I had been at our 'repetitions' here. I want it done *to the sound of the Waterfall.* I want the sound of the Waterfall louder and softer as the wind rises and falls, to be spoken through—like the music. I want the Waterfall *listened to when spoken of, and not looked out at.* The mystery and gloom of the scene would be greatly helped by this, and it would be new and picturesquely fanciful."

CHAPTER VIII.

DICKENS AS A DRAMATIC CRITIC.

In the interesting paper to which reference has already been made, that most excellent authority the late Mr. Dutton Cook, quoting chiefly from his letters,* speaks of Dickens as a dramatic critic, and many English playgoers will be relieved to find that he had not much sympathy with the methods in vogue at the world-famed Théâtre Français. Of this immaculate playhouse he wrote: "There is a dreary classicality at that establishment calculated to freeze the marrow. Between ourselves, even one's best friends there are at times aggravating. One tires of seeing a man, through any number of acts, remembering everything by patting his forehead with the flat of his hand, jerking out sentences by shaking himself, and piling them up in pyramids over his

---

* The writer might have followed the example of Mr. Dutton Cook, and have added to this chapter, on criticism from, the "letters"; but it seemed to him better to record the remaining dramatic extracts from these (and many of them are critical) in their own and separate place. See Cap. VII.

head with his right forefinger." And he relates of a generic small comedy piece, peculiar to the Français: "Where you see two sofas and three little tables, to which a man enters with his hat on to talk to another man—and in respect of which you know exactly when he will get up from one sofa to sit on the other, and take his hat off one table to put it upon the other—which strikes one quite as ludicrously as a good farce."

Dickens thoroughly disliked the "classical drama," and this led him to speak disparagingly of the acting of Rachel and Ristori. Indeed, he went so far as to declare that the famous "Medea" was "hopelessly bad"—and he was enthusiastic concerning Robson's acting in the travesty in which the performance was burlesqued.

Mr. Dutton Cook has more to tell of Dickens's opinion on the merits of French acting than of English, but he bears testimony to his undoubted and genuine admiration for Macready, speaks of his delight at Miss Woolgar's Lemuel in "The Green Bushes" at the Adelphi (long after, and as Mrs. Alfred Mellon, this excellent actress was the original Sally Goldstraw in "No Thoroughfare," on the same boards); tells the story of his pilgrimage to Walworth to see the amateur performance in which Mr. Toole figured, and recounts the great impression made upon him by Miss Marie Wilton's (Mrs. Bancroft's) early impersonations at the Strand.

Mr. Dutton Cook goes on to say :

"Of Mr. Emery's personation of Mr. Potter in 'Still Waters Run Deep' at the Olympic, in 1850, Dickens wrote: 'I don't think I ever saw anything meant to be funny that struck me as so extraordinarily droll; I couldn't get over it at all.' Of the William of T. P. Cooke in 'Black-Eye'd Susan,' Dickens wrote, congratulating the veteran upon his admirable performance, and adding: 'It was so fresh and vigorous, so manly and gallant, that I felt as if it splashed against my theatre-heated face along with the spray of the breezy sea.'

"In 1858 he was applauding Dr. Westland Marston's little drama, 'A Hard Struggle'; an excellent play, as good as 'La Joie fait Peur,' though not at all like it, with 'capital acting,' by Mr. Dillon. 'Real good acting, in imitation of nobody, and honestly made out by himself.' . . . It was in 1842 that Dickens had written a prologue for the same author's 'Patrician's Daughter,' produced at Drury Lane by Macready. 'Camilla's Husband,' at the Olympic in 1862, Dickens thought to be 'a very good play, very well played; real merit in Mr. Neville and Miss Saville.' In Fechter's management of the

Lyceum, commenced in 1863, Dickens took peculiar interest. The brilliant success of 'The Duke's Motto' thoroughly rejoiced his heart, and he specially noted Miss Kate Terry's performance in that play as 'perfectly charming; the very best piece of womanly tenderness he had ever seen on the stage.' Fechter's Hamlet, Dickens had from the first greatly admired. 'It was a performance of extraordinary merit, by far the most coherent, consistent, and intelligible Hamlet I ever saw. Some of the delicacies with which he rendered his conception clear were extremely subtle. . . . Add to this a perfectly picturesque and romantic " make up," and a remorseless destruction of all conventionalities, and you have the leading virtues of the impersonation. In Othello he did not succeed. In Iago he is very good. He is an admirable artist, and far beyond anyone on our stage.' In the production of 'The Master of Ravenswood,' Dickens took an active part, having, as he said, 'an earnest desire to put Scott, for once, upon the stage in his own gallant manner.' With the Lucy of Miss Carlotta Leclercq," (destined to be the heroine in " No Thoroughfare ") and " 'never thought of for Lucy, till all other Lucies had failed,' Dickens was extremely pleased. He found the actress 'marvellously good,' highly pathetic, and almost unrecognisable in person.

.... There is no one on the stage who could play the contract scene better or more simply and naturally, and I find it impossible to see it without crying.' With mention of Fechter's Claude Melnotte—in a letter to Lord Lytton—Dickens, says Mr. Dutton Cook, may be said to have closed his essays as a dramatic critic. 'Fechter has played nothing nearly so well as Claude since he played in Paris in the "Dame aux Camélias," or in London as Ruy Blas. He played the fourth act as finely as Macready, and the first act much better. The dress and bearing in the fifth act are quite new and excellent. ... I cannot say too much of the brightness, intelligence, picturesqueness, and care of Fechter's impersonation throughout. There was a remarkable delicacy in his gradually drooping down on his way home with his bride, until he fell upon the table a crushed heap of shame and remorse, while his mother told Pauline the story. His gradual recovery of himself as he formed better resolutions was equally well expressed; and his rising at last upright again and wishing enthusiastically to join the army, brought the house down.' . . . 'I wish you could have been there,' he wrote to the author. 'He never spoke English half so well as he spoke your English; and the audience heard it with the finest sympathy and respect. I felt that I should be very proud indeed to be the writer of the play.'"

Dickens naturally took keen interest in the famous Shakespearean revivals organised by Samuel Phelps at Sadler's Wells, and in writing to him on August 29th, 1847, he said:

"My dear Sir,—

"I cannot resist the impulse I feel to thank you for the very great pleasure I derived from the representation of 'Cymbeline' at your theatre on Thursday night. The excellent sense, taste, and feeling manifest throughout, the great beauty of all the stage arrangements, and the respectful consideration (so to speak) shown by every one concerned for the creation of the poet, gave me extraordinary gratification. Nor could I readily express to you, if I were to try, how strong a sense of the great service such a theatre renders to all who visit it, and to the general cause of literature and art.

"Even at the risk of seeming to intrude this sense upon you, I really cannot help assuring you of my warm interest and admiration. And perhaps you will receive my note with the greater favour when I confess to having resisted a similar impulse after several former visits to Sadler's

Wells, in my unwillingness to trouble you.

"Let me hope that I may have the pleasure of associating my public knowledge of you with a more private and personal one than hitherto, when I return to town in October; and believe me, my dear Sir,

"Faithfully yours,
"Charles Dickens."

Charles Dillon was another actor for whom Dickens entertained admiration. Writing to the eminent dramatist, Dr. Westland Marston, he said: "I have witnessed twice the representation of your charming little piece, 'A Hard Struggle.' . . . . . . You ask me what I think of Charles Dillon as an actor. His representation of *Reuben Holt* was exactly what acting should be—nature itself. I can't call to mind any living actor who could have played it so well. So closely did I watch him on both occasions that I could only discover one slight defect: on the receipt of the letter from his love announcing the arrival of Lilian, in his emotion he crumpled the paper in his hand. I think it would have been more consistent had he folded the letter carefully and placed it in his breast."

So highly did Dickens think of this play that

he suggested to his friend, Mons. Regnier, that he would do well to produce an adaptation of it at the Théâtre Français.

A play in which Dickens took great interest was the "Love's Martyrdom" of Mr. John Saunders, and in the author's preface to the published work, ample acknowledgment of this is made. Having submitted the work for his independent judgment, he received the following reply, and nothing could more conclusively prove the keen insight of Dickens as to the requirements of the stage:

"Tavistock House,
"Twenty-sixth October, 1854.
"DEAR SIR,—

"I have had much gratification and pleasure in the receipt of your obliging communication. Allow me to thank you for it, in the first place, with great cordiality.

"Although I cannot say that I came without any prepossessions to the perusal of your play (for I had favourable inclinations towards it before I begun), I *can* say that I read it with the closest attention, and that it inspired me with a strong interest and a genuine and high admiration. The parts that involved some of the greatest difficulties of your task appear to me those in which you shine most. I would particularly instance the end of Julia as a very striking example of this. The delicacy and beauty of her redemption from her weak, rash lover, are very far indeed beyond the range of any ordinary dramatist, and display the true poetical strength.

"As your hopes now centre in Mr. Phelps, and in seeing the child of your fancy on his stage, I will venture to point out to you, not only what I take to be very dangerous portions of 'Love's Martyrdom,' as it stands *for presentation on the stage*, but portions which I believe Mr. Phelps will speedily regard in that light, when he sees it before him in the persons of live men and women on the wooden boards. Knowing him, I think he will be as violently discouraged as he is now generously excited, and it may be useful to you to be prepared for the consideration of these passages.

"I do not regard it as a great stumbling-block that the play of modern times best known to an audience" (Sheridan Knowles's "Hunchback" was, of course, here alluded to) "proceeds upon the main idea of this, namely, that there was a hunchback who, because of his infirmity, mistrusted himself. But it is certainly a grain in the balance when the balance is going the wrong way, and therefore should be most carefully minimised. The incident of the ring is too insignificant to look at over a row of gas-lights, is difficult to convey to an audience, and the least thing will make it ludicrous. If it be so well done by Mr. Phelps himself as to be otherwise than ludicrous, it will be disagreeable. If it be either it will be perilous, and doubly so, because you revert to it. The quarrel scene between the two brothers in the third act is now so long, that the justification of blind passion and impetuosity, which can alone bear out Franklyn before the eyes of a great concourse of spectators, in plunging at the life of his own brother, is lost. That the two should be parted, and that Franklyn should again drive at him, and strike him, and then wound him, is a state of things to set the sympathy of the audience in the wrong direction, and turned from the man you make happy to the man you make unhappy. I would on no account allow the artist to appear attended by the picture more than once. All the most sudden inconsistency of Clarence I would soften down. Margaret must act much better than any actress I have ever seen if all her lines fall in pleasant places, therefore, I think she needs compression, too.

"All this applies solely to the theatre. If you revise the sheets for readers, will you note in the margin the broken laughter and the appeal to the Deity? If, in summing them up, you find you meant them, I would leave them as they stand by all means; if not, I would blot, accordingly.

"It is only in the hope of being slightly useful to you, by anticipating what I believe Mr. Phelps will discover, or what, if he should pass it by, I have a strong conviction the audience will find out, that I have ventured on these few hints. Your concurrence with them yourself, or re-consideration of your preference for the poem as it stands, cannot in the least affect my interest in your success. On the other hand, I have a perfect confidence in your not taking my misgivings ill. They arise solely out of my sincere desire for the triumph of your work.

"With renewed thanks for the pleasure you have given me, I am,

"Dear Sir,
"Faithfully yours,
"CHARLES DICKENS."

If every London theatre possessed a "reader" such as this, how many clever plays, written by brilliant writers, hampered with inexperience of stage-craft, might see the light! But, it must be owned, such readers are few and far between.

"Mr. Dickens," writes Mr. Saunders, "immediately took steps for the introduction of the drama to the theatre," and at the rehearsals, only four or five days before the performance, which was evidently not much more than a *succés d'éstime*, pointed out to the author "that the play was not then in so good a state as it would have been in Paris three weeks earlier."

The initial representation was given at the Haymarket Theatre, June, 1855, and in it Mr. Barry Sullivan, Mr. Howe, Mr. W. Farren, Miss Helen Faucit, and those time-honoured Haymarket Thespians, Messrs. Rogers, Braid, Weathersby, Coe and Clark took part.

Mr. James T. Fields, the American publisher and intimate friend of Dickens, says: "He was passionately fond of the theatre, loved the lights and music and flowers, and the happy faces of the audience. He was accustomed to say that his love of the theatre never failed, and, no matter how dull the play, he was always careful while he sat in the box to make no sound which could hurt the feelings of the actors, or show any lack of attention. His genuine enthusiasm for Mr. Fechter's acting was most interesting. He loved to describe seeing him first, quite by accident, in Paris, having strolled into a little theatre there one night. 'He was making love to a woman,' Dickens said, 'and he so elevated her as well as himself by the sentiment in which he enveloped her, that they trod in a purer ether, and in another sphere, quite lifted out of the present. By Heavens! I said to myself, a man who can do this can do anything. I never saw two people more purely and instantly elevated by the power of love. The manner also,' he continued, 'in which he presses the hem of the dress of Lucy, in the "Bride of Lammermoor," is something wonderful. The man has genius in him which is unmistakable.'"

When, early in 1870, Fechter left England for America, Dickens contributed to the *Atlantic Monthly* an article in his praise. "I cannot," said the novelist, "wish my friend a better audience than he will find in the American people, and I cannot wish them a better actor than they will find in my friend."

His admiration for Fechter's famous rendering of Hamlet is expressed in the following words:

"Perhaps no innovation in art was ever accepted with so much favour by so many intelligent persons, pre-committed to, and pre-occupied by, another system, as Fechter's Hamlet. I take this to have been the case (as it unquestionably was in London), not because of its picturesqueness, not because of its novelty, not because of its many scattered beauties, but because of its perfect consistency with itself. Its great and satisfying originality was in its possessing the merit of a distinctly conceived and executed idea. Fechter's Hamlet, a pale, woe-begone Norseman, with long flaxen hair, wearing a strange garb, never associated with the part upon the English stage (if ever seen there at all), and making a piratical swoop upon the whole fleet of little theatrical prescriptions without meaning, or like Dr. Johnson's celebrated friend, with only one idea in them, and that a wrong one, never could have achieved its extraordinary success but for its animation by one pervading purpose, to which all changes were made intelligently subservient."

CHAPTER IX.

CONCLUSION.

In this chapter the writer proposes to bring together sundry items without mention of which the record of the connection of Charles Dickens with the stage would hardly be complete, but which do not absolutely belong to any of the preceding divisions of the volume.

In Lady Pollock's "Macready as I knew him," mention is made of that great actor's admiration for Dickens. "Macready went on to dwell upon the genius of Dickens, upon his irresistible humour, his force, and his extraordinary powers of perception. 'What a marvellous describer Dickens is!' he said, with enthusiasm, 'how comprehensive his glance! What a power he has of penetrating his reader with his idea! I have laughed at Mr. F.'s aunt in "Little Dorrit," till I was nearly choked; and the lover's inventions for his own epitaph (in the same work) seemed to come home to me. I began to think I had composed the very same epitaph for myself, at some remote period of my life, of which I had forgotten the when and the how.'"

In the same interesting work we find that—
" In the latter days of Macready's life, when the weight of time and of sorrow pressed him down, Dickens was his most frequent visitor; he cheered him with narratives of bygone days; he poured some of his own abundant warmth into his heart; he led him into his own channels of thought; he gave readings to rouse his interest; he waked up in him again, by his vivid descriptions, his sense of humour—he conjured back his smile and his laugh."

That amusing book entitled "Glimpses of Real Life, as seen in the Theatrical World and in Bohemia, being the Confessions of Peter Paterson, a Strolling Comedian," published in 1864, contains the following appreciative dedication to Dickens:

To
CHARLES DICKENS, Esq.,
AUTHOR OF "NICHOLAS NICKLEBY,"
The Creator of Mr. Vincent Crummles,
and
"The Infant Phenomenon,"
THIS NARRATIVE,
In Admiration of that Gentleman's Literary Power,
IS RESPECTFULLY INSCRIBED
By his Humble Servant,
PETER PATERSON,
Strolling Player and Bohemian.

Speaking through the medium of his "Actor's Note-Book," of a dinner given by Sir James Moon, then Lord Mayor of London, to the members of the Garrick Club, on February 27th, 1855, Mr. George Vandenhoff, having previously complained of the dulness of the speeches, says: "Dickens was not present, or he would have redeemed its" (the Garrick Club's) "honour, and sent his hearers *smiling* to their beds."

In the first copies of the little volume of poems entitled "Infelicia," and published under the name of Adah Isaacs Menken of "Mazeppa" renown, the following letter from Dickens, to whom the book was dedicated, appeared in facsimile.

"Gad's Hill Place,
"Higham by Rochester, Kent,
"Monday, Twenty-First October, 1867.

"Dear Miss Menken,

"I shall have great pleasure in accepting your dedication, and I thank you for your portrait as a highly remarkable specimen of photography.

"I also thank you for the verses enclosed in your note. Many such enclosures come to me, but few so pathetically written, fewer still so modestly sent. "Faithfully yours,
"Charles Dickens."

Before many copies of the book were sold this letter was suppressed.

In Mr. Froude's "Thomas Carlyle; a History of His Life in London," will be found the following:—On April 29th, 1863, Carlyle wrote:

"I had to go yesterday to Dickens's Reading, 8 p.m., Hanover Rooms, to the complete upsetting of my evening habitudes and spiritual composure. Dickens does do it capitally, such as *it* is; acts better than any Macready in the world; a whole tragic, comic, heroic *theatre* visible performing under one *hat*, and keeping us laughing—in a sorry way, some of us thought—the whole night. He is a good creature, too, and makes fifty or sixty pounds by each of these readings."

In the "Dickens Chapter," comprised in his most entertaining "Recollections," Mr. Edmund Yates has much that is interesting to say of Dickens's fondness for the stage and, more particularly, of his liking for actors.

In the pleasant volume, entitled "Charles Dickens as I knew him," Mr. George Dolby has several things to tell of his "Chief," and his love for and connection with the stage, recording how "he worked incessantly with Fechter in the production of a sensational drama at the Lyceum entitled, 'The Long Strike,' by Dion Boucicault"; how when in one of the American theatres, the shortness of the ballet skirts was a source of such surprise to him, that in writing to Macready, he said: "Having some amiable talk with a neat little Spanish woman, who is the *première danseuse*, I asked her in a joke to let me measure her skirt with my dress glove. Holding the glove by the tip of the forefinger, I found the skirt to be just three gloves long, and yet its length was much in excess of the skirts of two hundred other ladies whom the carpenters were at that moment getting into their places for a transformation scene on revolving columns, or wires and 'travellers,' in wire cradles, up in the flies, down in the cellars, in every description of float that Wilmot, gone distracted, could imagine"; how, during this same American tour, and when "No Thoroughfare" had become an established success at the London Adelphi Theatre, all the American theatres were playing piratical versions of it; and although Mr. Dickens had, through Messrs. Ticknor and Fields, registered the play as their property (they being American citizens), still the managers defied the law, and continued playing the piece to overflowing houses. This was a source of annoyance to Mr. Dickens, less on account of the fees to which he considered himself entitled, than on account of the defiant manner in which his property was taken; notably in one case, in New York, when he proposed to a leading manager that he would be pleased to superintend the mounting of the piece in his theatre, if he would accept his services, and would use his own book rather than a mutilated one ; how, for the purpose of superintending the rehearsals of "No Thoroughfare," in its French dress, and "assisting" at its first representation at the Paris Vaudeville Theatre, Dickens went to the French capital, and returned highly delighted with the success of "L'Abîme," as it was then called; how Macready in his old age, and living in retirement at Cheltenham, came to one of the famous readings, and speaking to Dickens of his rendering of the terrible murder scene from "Oliver Twist," said : "You remember my best days, my dear boy ? No! that's not it. Well, to make a long story short, all I have to say is two Macbeths!" how "his interest in all that appertained to the theatrical world never left him, and one of the latest acts of his life was to correct an agreement for Miss Glynn (Mrs. Dallas) who had received offers to visit Australia, through the agency of the late Mr. E. P. Hingston, Artemus Ward's manager"; and finally how, at the readings given to the members of the theatrical profession, and into which he entered "with greater zest, I think, than into any others of the course"; he "wanted to show how much a single performer could do without the aid and stimulus of any of the ordinary adjuncts of the stage ; how many effects of a genuinely startling character could be produced without the help of scenery, costume, limelight, or mechanical contrivances."

"He succeeded," says Mr. Dolby (and no one could speak on the subject with greater authority), "to perfection, in the presence even of so thoroughly critical an audience. They applauded every point, cheering each well-known character, as the reader, by mere change of voice, manner and action, brought forward the people of his tales."

The writer is indebted to Mr. Fred G. Kitton for the following list of "Dickens's Theatrical Portraits":

As Captain Bobadil.	Woodcut drawn by Kenny Meadows. *Illustrated London News*, 1845.
Do.	Pen drawing by D. Maclise, R.A. with Forster as Kitely. Drawn on Play-bill. Re-produced in handbook of Dyce and Forster collections, South Kensington Museum.
Do.	Painting by C. R. Leslie, R.A., 1846. Engraved on wood, *Graphic*, August 26th, 1871.
As Aaron Gurnock.	In "The Lighthouse." Woodcut in *Illustrated London News*, July 21st, 1855.
Do.	And another in *Illustrated Times*, do.
As Sir Charles Coldstream.	In "Used Up." Painting by Augustus Egg, R.A. This was the property of Charles Dickens, and was sold by auction after the novelist's death.
As Richard Wardour.	In "The Frozen Deep." Cave scene. Woodcut, *Illustrated London News*, January 17th, 1857.

In Miss Kate Field's "Charles Albert Fechter," which is dedicated to "The Memory of Charles Dickens," and which forms a volume of the "American Actor Series," the old story of the friendship existing between the great English novelist and the famous French actor, and the admiration that the one felt for the other, is told over again. Miss Field is naturally eloquent concerning the successful production of "No Thoroughfare" in America, though, apparently, she has little faith in the amount of work that Dickens put into either the story or the play. "It is probable," she says, "that after talking over the plot together—a plot that is pre-eminently Collinsish—Dickens started the story, conceived the character of Joey Ladle, and, with a touch here and there, left the rest to his collaborateur." Miss Field also states that the version of "Belphegor" in which Fechter appeared at the Lyceum, was "entirely re-written by Charles Dickens, with a child's part introduced to display the great dramatic ability of Fechter's son Paul, then a child of seven."

The task that the writer set himself to perform is now at an end. He does not presume that he has exhausted his theme, for any subject with which the name of Charles Dickens is associated is, apparently, inexhaustible;—but if he has succeeded in directing attention to the enthusiastic interest that one of the greatest writers of the century took in the stage, and the well-being of the stage ; if he has pointed out more directly, or more collectively, than has been pointed out before the influence that his name and works have had and hold upon the stage ; or if, finally, he has caused any single reader an enjoyment in the perusal of his pages equal to that which he has taken in their compilation, his labour will not have been in vain.

INDEX.

Aaron Gurnock 252
"A Christmas Carol" 155, 157, 169, 171
Addison, Mr. 183
"Adrienne Lecouvreur" ... 219
"A Good Night's Rest" 100
"A Hard Struggle" ...234, 238
Albery, Mr. James 182
Alfred Jingle 12, 13, 142, 152, 181, 182
"All for Her" 174
Allison, Miss 85
"All the Year Round" 89
Almar, Mr. George 161
"American Actor Series" ... 253
"A Midsummer Night's Dream" 215
"An Actor's Note Book" 180, 248
"A National Theatre" 213
"Animal Magnetism" 113
Archer, Mr. 181
"A Roland for an Oliver" ... 98
"Artemus Ward" 251
"Astley's" 11, 227
"As You Like It" 219
"A Tale of Two Cities" 131, 174
Athenæum, The 178, 179
Atlantic Monthly 244
Attwood, Mr 142
Auber 219

Bancroft, Mrs. 234
"Bardell v. Pickwick" 153, 157
Barnett, Mr. M 83
Bartley, Mr 94, 96
Beaumont and Fletcher 103
Bell, Mr. Robert 117
Belmore, Mr. George 150, 154, 174
"Belphegor" 253
Belvawney Miss 23
Bennett, Mr 83
Bentley's Miscellany 122
Billington, Mr. John 173

Billington, Mrs 174
Birmingham 103
"Black-Eyed Susan" 79, 207, 234
"Bleak House" 48, 50, 179, 180
"Boots at the Holly-Tree Inn" 157
Boucicault, Mr. Dion 173, 212, 249
Boyle, Miss Mary ...132, 209, 221
"Boz and the Play" 89
Braham Mr. 83, 84, 88, 97, 201, 202
Braid, Mr. 243
Bravassa, Miss 23, 27, 37
Brooks, Mr. Shirley 130
Brough, Mr. Lionel 155, 180, 181
Buckstone, Mr. 80
Burnett, Mr. 180
Byron, Mr. H. J. 173

Caffery, Mr. Stephen 183
"Camilla's Husband" 234
Campden House 124
Captain Bobadil ...109, 111, 252
Carlton Chronicle 86, 87
Carlyle, Thomas 127, 249
Celeste, Madame 132
Cerjat, Mons. de 210
Chapman and Hall ... 3, 118, 206
"Charles Dickens as a Reader" 99
"Charles Dickens as I knew him" 249
Chéri, Madame Rose 211
"Clarissa Harlowe" 211
Clark, Mr. 243
Clarke, Mrs. Cowden 101, 102, 103, 104, 106, 108, 109, 110, 128
Clarke, Mr. John 150, 154, 155, 156, 157, 180
Clarke, Mr. John S. 150
Claude Melnotte 236
"Claudian" 168, 169
Clayton, Mr. John 174, 175
Clifford, Mrs 80
Coe, Mrs 117, 118

INDEX.

Coe, Mr. 118, 243
Cole, Mr. 101
Collette, Mr. Charles 175
Collier, Mr. John Payne 102
Collins, Mr. Charles 130, 131
Collins, Mr. Wilkie .... 89, 91, 92, 93, 117, 118, 124, 125, 128, 130, 220, 253.
"Comfortable Lodgings" ... 100
Compton, Mr. Edward 180
Compton, Mrs. Henry, 117, 134, 135
Cook, Mr. Dutton............. 96, 232, 233, 234. 236
Cooke, Mr. T. P. 207, 234
Costello, Mr. Dudley 101, 116, 118
Coulson, Mr. 84
Coutts, Mr...................... 80
Cruikshank, George 101, 102
Cunningham, Mr. Peter. 102, 117
Curdle, Mr. 28, 29, 46
Curdle, Mrs................. 28, 30
Cushman, Miss Charlotte ... 180
"Cymbeline" 237

Dallas, Mrs. 251
Daly, Miss....................... 142
"David Copperfield" 48, 176, 184, 185
"Deaf as a Post"................ 98
Devonshire, The Duke of ... 117
Devonshire House..........116, 119
Dickens, Mr. Alfred............ 130
Dickens, Mr. Augustus 101
Dickens, Mrs. Charles ...113, 211
Dickens, Mr. Charles, Junr.. 91, 124, 130
Dickens, Mr. Frederick 101, 102, 113
"Dickensiana"............157, 168
Dillon, Mr. Charles 234, 238
Dolby, Mr. George.........249, 252
"Dombey and Son" 48, 162, 176, 177
Dramatic, Equestrian and Musical Fund 191
"Dr. Marigold" 173
Drummond, Miss Dolores ... 180
Dumas, Alexandre 206, 220
Eaton, Mr......................... 102
Edinburgh 103
Egg, Mr. Augustus, R.A...... 101, 102, 113, 117, 118, 129, 130, 252
Eldred, Mr. Joseph 175

Emery, Mr. S. 150, 155, 160, 176, 177, 234
"English to the Core" 212
Ernstone, Miss 176
"Every Man in His Humour" 100, 101, 104, 107, 109, 112

Fanny Dorrit.........51, 52, 54, 55
Farren, Mr........................ 79
Farren, Miss Nellie 179
Farren, Mr. William......178, 243
Faucit, Miss Helen 243
"Faust" 225
Fechter, Mons. Charles 17, 91, 92, 174, 223, 225, 226, 228, 230, 234, 235, 236, 243, 244, 253
Felton, Professor 203, 205
Fernandez, Mr. James ...150, 175
Field, Miss Kate 253
Fielding, Henry.................. 123
Fields, Mr. James T............ 243
Fisher, Mr. David................ 175
Fitzgerald, Mr. Percy ... 175, 184
Fitzpatrick, Mr.................. 152
Florence, Mr..................... 177
Folair, Mr............22, 24, 25, 32
Foote, Miss Lydia 150
Forester, Mr..................... 84, 85
Forster, Mr. John............... 16, 89, 90, 94, 96, 98, 101, 102, 112, 113, 115, 117, 122, 136, 137, 158, 170, 206, 213, 221, 226, 227, 252
Fortescue, Miss 101, 136
Fraser's Magazine 163
Frederick Dorrit......... 13, 51, 54
Froude, Mr. 249

Gad's Hill................14, 127, 128
Gallery of Illustration 129
Gardner, Mr. 83, 84, 85
Gazingi, Miss 23
General Theatrical Fund Association 194, 197
Gentleman's Magazine 119
Gilbert, Mr. W. S. 88, 174
Glasgow 103
"Glimpses of Real Life, etc." 247
Glover, Mrs. 80
Glynn, Miss 251
Goldsmith, Oliver............... 103

INDEX.

Gough, Mr. 80
Gower, Miss 149
"Great Expectations" 55, 172, 174
Grimaldi Joseph 15, 16
Grudden, Mrs. 23
Guild of Literature and Art 114, 116, 118
Hale, Mr. Henry 113
Hall, Mr. H. 142
Halliday, Mr. Andrew 137, 150, 176
"Hamlet" 235, 244, 248
Hammond, Mr. 141
Hammond, Mrs. 142
Hanover Square Rooms 116, 249
"Hard Times" 77, 78
Hare, Mr. John 86
Harley, Mr. J. P. 83, 84, 85, 87, 202, 206, 212
Hazlitt, William 195
Hawkins, Mr. Henry 112
"Heart's Delight" 176
Herman, Mr. H. 168, 169
Hingston, Mr. E. P. 251
Hogarth, Miss 113, 216
Hollingsworth, Mr. 84
Horne, Mr. R. H. 117, 119, 121, 205
Howe, Mr. 79, 183, 243
Hullah, Mr. John 83, 88, 201, 205
Humby, Mrs. 80
Hunt, Leigh 100

Inchbald, Mrs. 113
"Infelicia" 248
"In the French Flemish Country" 66
Irving, Mr. Henry 12, 152, 181, 182
"Is She His Wife?" 2, 82, 85

"Jane Osborne" 216
Jem Hutley 13, 14
Jerrold, Blanchard 79
Jerrold, Douglas 79, 103, 113, 116, 129, 130
Joey Ladle 90, 91
John 14
Jonson, Ben ... 100, 101, 102, 112
Journal of a London Playgoer 124
Justice Shallow 103, 108, 110

Kean, Charles 188
Keeley, Robert 154, 155, 160, 161, 207, 210, 211

Keeley, Mrs. 136, 149, 150, 153, 154, 155, 161, 163, 178, 207, 210, 211
Kelly, Miss 215
Kendal, Mr. 86
Kendal, Mrs. 86, 183
Kent, Mr. Charles 99
Kenworthy, Miss 101
Kitton, Mr. Fred G. 157, 158, 168, 252
Knebworth 112, 114
Knight, Mr. Charles 102, 117
Knowles, Sheridan 240

L'Abîme 251
Lacy, Mr. W. 79
"La Dame aux Camelias" ... 236
"La Joie Fait Peur" ... 216, 234
Lane, Mrs. Sarah 73
Leclercq, Miss Carlotta 235
Ledbrook, Miss 23
Lee, Mr. 142
Lee, Miss Jennie 179, 180
Leech, John 101, 113
Lenville, Mr. 22, 23, 24, 25, 27, 32, 33, 37
Lenville, Mrs. 23
Lemaitre, Mons. 217, 218
Lemon, Mark 89, 101, 102, 103, 113, 115, 117, 118, 120, 122, 123, 129, 130, 135
Lemon, Mrs. Mark 113
Leslie, C. R. R.A. 252
"Letters of Elizabeth Barrett Browning" 119
Lewes, Mr. G. H. 101, 102
"Little Dorrit" 51, 52, 53, 54, 162, 236
"Little Em'ly" 176, 184
"*Little Swills*" ... 48, 49, 50, 51
Liverpool 100, 103
London Assurance 212
London Tavern 197
Longman's Magazine 96
Lord Wilmot 116, 121
Lotta, Miss 154
"Love, Law and Physic" ... 102, 103, 107, 110
"Love's Martyrdom" 239, 240, 241, 242

17

INDEX.

Lytton Sir E. Bulwer (afterwards Lord) 103, 112, 115, 116, 199, 214, 221, 222, 229, 236
Maclise, D. R.A. 252
Macmillan's Magazine 132
Macready, W. C. 17, 80, 81, 97, 99, 162, 199, 202, 204, 205, 210, 215, 225, 233, 234, 236, 237, 246, 247, 249, 251
Manchester............100, 103, 129
Marston, Dr. Westland 117, 204, 234, 238
"Martin Chuzzlewit" 47, 154, 177, 178, 207
Mathews, Mr. C. 97
Mathews, Mr. Frank 155
Mathews, Mrs. Frank 155
May, Mr. 84
"Mazeppa" 227, 248
Meadows, Mr. 155, 160
Meadows, Kenny 252
Melbourne, Lord 112
Mellon, Mr. 80
Mellon, Mrs. Alfred........... 150, 174, 228, 233
Melvilleson, Miss M. 50
"Memoirs of Joseph Grimaldi" 15, 16
Menken, Miss Ada Isaacs 227, 248
Merivale, Herman............... 174
Moncrieff, Mr. William 137, 142, 143, 148
"Money" 103, 214, 221
Morley, Mr. Henry 124
Montague, Miss Emmeline 134, 135
Montreal 98, 203
"Mr. Nightingale's Diary" ... 89, 116, 118, 122
"Mrs. Joseph Porter" 9

Neville, Mr. Henry 131, 174, 234
"Nicholas Nickleby" 17, 18, 19, 20, 21, 22, 24, 26, 28, 29, 30, 31, 32, 33, 34, 35, 36, 38, 39, 40, 41, 42, 43, 44, 45, 46, 143, 144, 145, 146, 147, 148, 149, 150, 151, 163, 164, 165, 166, 167, 168, 247
"Not so Bad as We Seem" 116, 118, 121, 214

"No Thoroughfare" 16, 89, 90, 91, 93, 173, 230, 233, 235, 250, 251, 253
Obenreizer 90, 91, 92
"Old Drury Lane" 148
"Oliver Twist" 157, 161, 162, 163, 173, 251
O'Neil Miss........................ 149
"Othello" 235

Paris 163, 216, 217, 220, 225, 250
Parry, Mr. John 83, 84
"Past Two o'clock in the Morning" 98
Paterson, Peter 247
Paxton, Sir Joseph 120
Penson, Mrs....................... 84
Petowker, Miss 30, 31
Phelps, Mr. Samuel 237, 240, 241, 242
Pigott, Mr. Edward 130
Pip, Mr. 47, 48
Pollock, Lady..................... 246
Portraits........................ 252
"Principles of Comedy and Dramatic Effect" 184
"Private Theatres" 5
P. Saloy Family ... 66, 67, 68, 69
Punch 177

Rachel 219, 233
Radcliffe, Mr. F.P. Delmé 112, 113
Rainforth, Miss 83, 88
Regnier, Mons 132, 213, 215, 239
"Reprinted Pieces"............ 77
Richardson, Mr. A. 142
Richardson, Samuel 211, 212
Richard Wardour ...130, 131, 252
Righton, Mr. Edward 173
Rimmer, Mr. Alfred............ 22
Ristori............................ 233
Roberts, D., R.A. 117
Robson, F. 128, 233
Rogers, Mr. 243
Romer, Miss Anne 102, 113
Rowe, Mr. 175, 176
"Royal Dramatic College" 188, 189
"Ruy Blas" 236

Sabine, Miss Ellen 130
Sadler's Wells 237, 238

INDEX. 259

	PAGE
Sala, Madame	84, 85
Sally Goldstraw	90
"Sam Weller"	137, 145
Saunders, Mr. John	239, 240, 242
Saville, Miss	234
Scribe	219
Shepherd, Mr. R. H.	89
Sidney, Mr.	84
"Sikes and Nancy"	157
Simpson, Mr. J. Palgrave	174
Sir Charles Coldstream	110, 252
Sir Epicure Mammon	102
"Sketches by Boz"	5, 11, 98
"Sleary's Horsemanship"	77
Sleary, Mr.	78
Smike	19, 22
Smith, Albert	158
Smith, Miss A.	80
Smith, Miss Julia	83, 84
Smith Mr. O.	136, 149
Snittle Timberry	39, 41
Snevellicci, Miss	23, 27, 28, 30, 35, 36
South Kensington Museum	94, 252
Stanfield, Clarkson, R.A.	117, 119, 125, 127, 130, 207
Stephens, Mrs. Jane	179
"Still Waters Run Deep"	234
Stirling, Mrs.	194
Stirling, Mr. Edward	148, 151, 152, 153, 154, 155, 156
Stone, Mr. Frank	101, 113, 116
Stratford-on-Avon	101
Strickland, Mr.	83
Sullivan, Mr. Barry	243
Sydney Carton	132
Talfourd, Sergeant	81
Tavistock House	122
Taylor, Tom	132
Telbin, Mr.	117, 130
Tennent, Sir James Emmerson	220
Tenniel, Mr. John	117
Ternan, Mrs.	130
Ternan, Miss Ellen	130
Ternan, Miss Maria	130
Terriss, Mr. W.	150
Terry, Mr. Edward	175
Terry, Miss Kate	225, 235
Thackeray W. M.	163, 164, 165, 166, 167, 168
"The Alchemist"	102

	PAGE
The Almanack of The Month	158
Theatres—Adelphi	17, 89, 90, 91, 93, 148, 153, 163, 189, 228, 233, 250
Ambigu Comique	163, 217
Britannia (Hoxton)	72, 73, 74, 75, 76
City of London	152
Court	174
Covent Garden	17, 96, 212, 221
Drury Lane	186, 199, 202, 234
Haymarket	101, 103, 243
Lyceum	132, 154, 158, 181, 183, 226, 235, 248, 253
Olympic	128, 131, 184, 234
Opéra Comique (Boulogne)	216
Opéra Comique (Paris)	219
Porte St. Martin	216, 220
Portsmouth	21, 22
Princess's	187, 227
St. James's	83, 85, 86, 87, 202, 206, 215
Strand	137, 143, 150, 230, 234
Surrey	161, 162
Théâtre Français	69, 132, 216, 232, 239
Vaudeville	177, 178
Vaudeville (Paris)	251
Theatre Magazine	89
"The Battle of Life"	210, 211
"The Best of all Good Company"	79
"The Bride of Lammermoor"	244
"The Captives"	229
"The Chimes"	172
"The Cricket on the Hearth"	158, 172, 173, 183
"The Compact Enchantress"	77
"The Courier of Lyons"	226
"The Duke's Motto"	235
"The Frozen Deep"	128, 129, 130, 131, 252
The Garrick Club	248
"The Good Natured Man"	103
"The Great Winglebury Duel"	206
"The Green Bushes"	233

INDEX.

"The Haunted Man" 172
"The Hunchback" 240
The Infant Phenomenon... 22, 24, 29, 247
"The Lady of Lyons" 222, 223, 228, 236
"The Lamplighter"....... 94, 202
"The Lighthouse" 124, 125, 128, 252
"The Long Strike" 249
"*The Mask*" 93
"The Master of Ravenswood" 235
"The Merchant of Venice"... 188
"The Merry Wives of Windsor" 103, 104
"The Old Curiosity Shop" 153
"The Patrician's Daughter" 204, 234
"The Pickwick Papers" ... 12, 138, 139, 152, 157, 181, 183
"The Rent Day" 103
"The Rivals" 209
"The Strange Gentleman" 2, 82, 84, 86, 87, 203
"The Streets of London" ... 227
"The Stroller's Tale" 13
"The Uncommercial Traveller" 66, 69
"The Village Coquettes" ... 2, 82, 83, 85, 87, 201, 205
"The White Rose" 223, 224
"Thirty Years of a Gambler's Life" 217
Thorne, Mr. Thomas...... 155, 178
Ticknor and Fields 250
"Time Works Wonders" ... 79
Tom Pinch 177
Toole, Mr. J. L. 153, 170, 171, 172, 173, 228, 233
Topham, Mr. F. W. 117
Tully Mr. 152
Turner, Miss 160
Turner, Mr. Godfrey 89
"Turning the Tables" 100

"Two Views of a Cheap Theatre" 69, 70, 71, 72, 73, 74, 75, 76
"Used Up" 110, 252

Vandenhoff, Mr. George 180, 248
Vestris, Madame 212
Viardot, Madame 225
Vincent Crummles.............. 13, 17, 18, 19, 21, 22, 23, 24, 26, 31, 32, 33, 34, 35, 37, 38, 39, 40, 41, 45, 46, 122, 142, 247
Vincent Crummles, Mrs......... 22, 23, 31, 32, 37, 39
Vining, Mr. F. 155, 160
Vining, Mrs. George............ 130

Waugh, Colonel................... 124
Weathersby, Mr. 243
Webster, Mr. Benjamin 80, 81, 82, 91, 174
Wigan, Mr. Alfred 155
Wilkinson, Mr. 149, 152, 163
Williamson, Mr. 84
Willis's Rooms 191
Willmott, Mr. 101
Wilson, Mr. Effingham William 213
Wilton, Miss Marie 234
Woolgar, Miss 155, 233
Wopsle, Mr. 13, 55, 56, 57, 58, 59, 60, 61, 62, 63, 64, 65, 66
Worthing 151
Woulds, Miss.................... 102
Wright, Mr. 136
Wyatt, Mr. Frank................ 154

Yates, Mr. Edmund............ 249
Yates, Mr. F. 97, 136, 149, 153, 163
York, The Hon. Eliot 113
Young, Miss 117, 118
Younge, Mr............... 142, 155

Mr. Redway's Bibliographical Publications.

HINTS TO COLLECTORS of Original Editions of the Works of CHARLES DICKENS. By CHARLES PLUMPTRE JOHNSON. Printed on hand-made paper, and bound in vellum. Crown 8vo., 6s.

"Enthusiastic admirers of Dickens are greatly beholden to Mr. C. P. Johnson for his useful and interesting 'Hints to Collectors of Original Editions of the Works of Charles Dickens' (Redway). The book is a companion to the similar guide to collectors of Thackeray's first editions, is compiled with the like care, and produced with the like finish and taste."—*The Saturday Review.*

THE BIBLIOGRAPHY OF SWINBURNE; a Bibliographical list, arranged in chronological order, of the published writings in Verse and Prose of ALGERNON CHARLES SWINBURNE (1857-1887). Revised and enlarged edition, in crown 8vo., parchment, price 6s.

* *Only* 250 *Copies Printed.*

Literary and Historical Edition of Poe's Raven.

THE RAVEN, by EDGAR ALLAN POE. With Variorum Readings, and a Literary and Historical Commentary. By JOHN H. INGRAM. Embracing the genesis and history, the translations into French, German, Hungarian and Latin, the fabrications and parodies, and the bibliography of the most popular lyrical poem in the world. Crown 8vo., parchment, gilt top, uncut, price 3s. 6d.

TOBACCO TALK AND SMOKERS' GOSSIP. An Amusing Miscellany of Fact and Anecdote relating to "The Great Plant" in all its Forms and Uses, including a Selection from Nicotian Literature. Bound in fancy cloth, uncut edges. Price 2s.

"One of the best books of gossip we have met for some time. . . . It is literally crammed full from beginning to end of its 148 pages with well-selected anecdotes, poems, and excerpts from tobacco literature and history."—*Graphic.*
"The smoker should be grateful to the compilers of this pretty little volume. . . . No smoker should be without it, and anti-tobacconists have only to turn over its leaves to be converted "—*Pall Mall Gazette.*
"Something to please smokers; and non-smokers may be interested in tracing the effect of tobacco—the fatal, fragrant herb—on our literature."—*Literary World.*

GEORGE REDWAY, YORK STREET, COVENT GARDEN.

The only Published Biography of John Leech.

JOHN LEECH, Artist and Humourist. A Biographical Sketch, by FRED. G. KITTON. An édition de luxe in demy 18mo, cloth, price 1s.

"In the absence of a fuller biography we cordially welcome Mr. Kitton's interesting little sketch."—*Notes and Queries.*
"The multitudinous admirers of the famous artist will find this touching monograph well worth careful reading and preservation."—*Daily Chronicle.*
"The very model of what such a memoir should be."—*Graphic.*

Ebenezer Jones's Poems.

STUDIES OF SENSATION AND EVENT, by EBENEZER JONES. Edited by RICHARD HERNE SHEPHERD, with Memorial Notices of the Author by SUMNER JONES and W. J. LINTON. In Post 8vo, with portrait, cloth, old style. Price 5s.

"This remarkable poet affords nearly the most striking instance of neglected genius in our modern school of poetry. His poems are full of vivid disorderly power."—D. G. ROSSETTI.

WELLERISMS FROM "PICKWICK" AND "MASTER HUMPHREY'S CLOCK." Selected by CHARLES F. RIDEAL. Edited, with an Introduction, by CHARLES KENT, Author of "The Humour and Pathos of Charles Dickens." Demy 18mo., 200 pages, cloth, uncut. Price 2s.

"Some write well, but he writes Weller."—*Epigram on Dickens.*
"Some of the best sayings of the immortal Sam and his sportive parent are collected here. The book may be taken up for a few minutes with the certainty of affording amusement, and it can be carried away in the pocket."—*Literary World.*
"It was a very good idea . . . . the extracts are very humourous . . . here nothing is missed."—*Glasgow Herald.*

DICKENSIANA. A Bibliography of the Literature relating to CHARLES DICKENS and his Writings. Compiled by FRED. G. KITTON, with a portrait of "Boz," from a Drawing by SAMUEL LAURENCE. 544 pages, Crown 8vo., green cloth boards, price 10s. (Only 500 copies printed—a few remain.)

"DICKENSIANA."
"If with your Dickens lore you'd make
Considerable headway,
The way to be well-read's to take
This book brought out by REDWAY.
'Tis clear, exhaustive, and compact,
Both well arranged and written;
A mine of anecdote and fact,
Compiled by F. G. KITTON."—*Punch.*

Mr. Swinburne's New Poem.

A WORD FOR THE NAVY, by ALGERNON CHARLES SWINBURNE. Edition limited to 250 copies, each numbered. Price 5s.

GEORGE REDWAY, YORK STREET, COVENT GARDEN.

AN ESSAY ON THE GENIUS OF GEORGE CRUIKSHANK, by "THETA" (WILLIAM MAKEPEACE THACKERAY). With all the original Woodcut Illustrations, a New Portrait of CRUIKSHANK, etched by PAILTHORPE, and a Prefatory Note on THACKERAY AS AN ART CRITIC, by W. E. CHURCH. A few large-paper copies, with India proof portrait, in imperial 8vo., parchment paper covers. Price 7s. 6d.

"Thackeray's essay 'On the Genius of George Cruikshank,' reprinted from the *Westminster Review*, is a piece of work well calculated to drive a critic of these days to despair. How inimitable is its touch! At once familiar and elegant, serious and humorous, enthusiastically appreciative, and yet just and clear-sighted; but, above all, what the French call *personnel*. It is not the impersonnel reviewer who is going through his paces . . . it is Thackeray talking to us as few can talk—talking with apparent carelessness, even ramblingly, but never losing the thread of his discourse, or saying a word too much, nor ever missing a point which may help to elucidate his subject or enhance the charm of his essay. . . . Mr. W. E. Church's prefatory note on 'Thackeray as an Art Critic' is interesting and carefully compiled."—*Westminster Review*, Jan. 15th.

"As the original copy of the *Westminster* is now excessively rare, this re-issue will, no doubt, be welcomed by collectors."—*Birmingham Daily Mail*.

"The new portrait of Cruikshank by F. W. Pailthorpe is a clear, firm etching."—*The Artist*.

HINTS TO COLLECTORS OF ORIGINAL EDITIONS OF THE WORKS OF WILLIAM MAKEPEACE THACKERAY, by CHARLES PLUMPTRE JOHNSON. Printed on hand-made paper and bound in vellum. Crown 8vo., 6s.

". . . . A guide to those who are great admirers of Thackeray, and are collecting first editions of his works. The dainty little volume, bound in parchment and printed on hand-made paper, is very concise and convenient in form; on each page is an exact copy of the title-page of the work mentioned thereon, a collation of pages and illustrations, useful hints on the differences in editions, with other matters indispensable to collectors. . . . . Altogether it represents a large amount of labour and experience."—*The Spectator*.

SEA-SONG AND RIVER-RHYME, from Chaucer to Tennyson. Selected and Edited by ESTELLE DAVENPORT ADAMS. With a new Poem by ALGERNON CHARLES SWINBURNE. With Twelve Etchings. Large crown 8vo, cloth, top edge gilt, 10s. 6d.

"The book is, on the whole, one of the best of its kind ever published.—*Glasgow Herald*.

"The editor has made the selection with praiseworthy judgment."—*Morning Post*

"Twelve really exquisite and delicately executed etchings of sea and river-side accompany and complete this beautiful volume."—*Morning Post*.

"A special anthology delightful in itself and possessing the added graces of elegant printing and dainty illustrations."—*Scotsman*.

"The volume is got up in the handsomest style, and includes a dozen etchings of sea and river scenes, some of which are exquisite."—*Literary World*.

GEORGE REDWAY, YORK STREET, COVENT GARDEN.

Newly-Discovered Poem by Charles Lamb

BEAUTY AND THE BEAST; OR, A ROUGH OUTSIDE WITH A GENTLE HEART, by CHARLES LAMB. Now first reprinted from the Original Edition of 1811, with Preface and Notes, by RICHARD HERNE SHEPHERD. Only 100 Copies printed. Fcap. 8vo., printed on handsome paper at the Chiswick Press, and bound in parchment by Burn to form a companion volume to " Tamerlane." Price 10s. 6d.

SULTAN STORK, and other Stories and Sketches. By WILLIAM MAKEPEACE THACKERAY (1829-1844). Now first collected. To which is added THE BIBLIOGRAPHY OF THACKERAY, Revised and Considerably Enlarged. Demy 8vo., cloth, 10s. 6d.

(Uniform with the new " Standard " Edition of Smith, Elder and Co.)

" Admirers of Thackeray may be grateful for a reprint of ' Sultan Stork.' "—*Athenæum.*

" A handsome volume."—*Glasgow Herald.*

" Thackeray collectors, however, have only to be told that none of the pieces now printed appear in the two volumes recently issued by Messrs. Smith, Elder and Cc., in order to make them desire their possession. They will also welcome the revision of the Bibliography, since it now presents a complete list, arranged in chronological order, of Thackeray's published writings in prose and verse, and also of his sketches and drawings."—*Daily Chronicle.*

" We do not assume to fix/ Mr. Thackeray's rank or to appraise his merits as an art critic. We only know that, in our opinion, few of his minor writings are so pleasant to read as his shrewd and genial comments on modern painters and paintings."—*Saturday Review.*

FORTUNATE LOVERS (The). Twenty-seven novels of the Queen of Navarre. Translated from the original French by ARTHUR MACHEN. Edited and selected from the Heptameron, with Notes, Pedigrees, and an Introduction. By A. MARY F. ROBINSON. With Original Etching by G. P. Jacomb-Hood. Large crown 8vo., cloth, illuminated, top edge gilt, 10s. 6d.

"Super-realistic as the love stories now and then are, according to our notions of modesty, they have one and all a wholesome moral, and go far to throw light on an interesting period in the history of France. Handsomely bound and ' got up,' and furnished with a charming etching by Mr. Jacomb-Hood as frontispiece, the volume may well be recommended to all readers, and particularly to all students of history."—*Pall Mall Gazette.*

" Miss Robinson's notes, and more especially her ably-written Introduction, which is practically a biography of Margaret of Angoulême, will enable readers to appreciate the ' personalities' in the stories more keenly than would otherwise be possible."—*Scotsman.*

GEORGE REDWAY, YORK STREET. COVENT GARDEN.

www.ingramcontent.com/pod-product-compliance
Lightning Source LLC
Chambersburg PA
CBHW031943230426
43672CB00010B/2027